I10637682

HEALING TOUCH

HEALING TOUCH

The Church's Forgotten Language

Zach Thomas

Westminster/John Knox Press
Louisville, Kentucky

© 1994 Zach Thomas

All rights reserved. No part of this book may be reproduced or transmitted in any form or by any means, electronic or mechanical, including photocopying, recording, or by any information storage or retrieval system, without permission in writing from the publisher. For information, address Westminster/John Knox Press, 100 Witherspoon Street, Louisville, Kentucky 40202-1396.

Scripture quotations from the New Revised Standard Version of the Bible are copyright © 1989 by the Division of Christian Education of the National Council of the Churches of Christ in the U.S.A. and are used by permission.

Book design by Drew Stevens

Cover design by Laura Lee

First edition

Published by Westminster/John Knox Press
Louisville, Kentucky

This book is printed on acid-free paper that meets the American National Standards Institute Z39.48 standard.⊗

PRINTED IN THE UNITED STATES OF AMERICA
9 8 7 6 5 4 3 2 1

Library of Congress Cataloging-in-Publication Data

Thomas, Zach, date.
    Healing touch : the church's forgotten language / Zach Thomas.—
1st ed.
      p.   cm.
    Includes bibliographical references and index.
    ISBN 0–664–25187–0 (alk. paper)
    1. Spiritual healing.   2. Touch—Religious aspects—Christianity.
3. Pastoral theology.   I. Title.
BT732.5.T474   1994
253'.7—dc20   93–46595

To Mom and Dad
Sally and Leigh
and the
Seigle Avenue
Presbyterian Church

Contents

Foreword

This is a remarkable book. The author, a Presbyterian minister, has made an extensive study of the power of touch in human healing. In his own journey toward wholeness, he discovered anew how faith, hope, and love are the basic elements in the healing process. Then, quite by accident, he experienced healing touch himself. This experience spurred him to travel to other cultures to learn from persons who give primary attention to massage and human touch in their healing arts.

Thomas is convinced that touch and anointing are part of the scripture's attention to holistic health and cites the emphasis of Hebrew prophets and New Testament personalities on holistic health, shalom. He then traces the decline of these procedures through history and notes that the church became more in touch with intellectual concepts than with physical touch. He believes that the time is at hand for a recovery of our original heritage.

Fortunately, in our time there is evidence that touching is once again seen as a healing force. Thomas uses the phrase, "heart/hand coordination" to place a healing dimension in bodywork. He describes how touch can become a part of vital and personal pastoral care.

Thomas notes that referral is often indicated for the welfare of the client or parishioner. He cautions that care needs to be taken in identifying the person to whom the referral is to be made. In addition, he notes that clear reasons need to be given to the client for the referral. He advises that it is important to match a person's need with the appropriate type of professional and provides guidelines for this process.

In concluding his discussion, Thomas turns his attention to the use of healing touch in worship. He notes that very few occasions are ordinarily provided for such activity except for the ordination of church leaders and clergy. He discusses criteria and guidelines to be used in the incorporation of touch in worship. Layfolk and pastors need encouragement to reclaim profoundly meaningful ways to practice the laying on of hands in gatherings of the congregation. Just because this gesture has been coopted by various cultural and cultic powers is no reason for the church to abandon something so integral to its mission.

The biblically based concepts of health and wholeness, healing process, and heart/hand coordination should be studied in seminaries. I would like to see his model for examining touch in pastoral episodes used by any group that wants to train its members to embody compassion more effectively. The book will complement other resources now appearing so that healing touch might once again play a role in the church's response to its members' ongoing need for pastoral care.

Thomas closes with an epilogue that is moving and very meaningful. He tells of a visit to a museum in Bangkok, Thailand, where he saw a sculpture of the sleeping Vishnu, attended by two celestial helpers. When asked why the helpers were massaging the legs of Vishnu, the guide answered, "Well, it's going to take Vishnu a long time to dream a new world. He'll need lots of healing energy."

He concludes: "One hopes we will be more like the helpers at Vishnu's legs or like Jesus washing the disciples' feet. By laying on hands we do not will*fully* inflate our grandiosity, nor do we will-*less*ly freeze in the face of evil. Rather, we will*ing*ly provide the compassion and energy it takes to live toward visions of shalom only the Creator can give."

William B. Oglesby, Jr.
Professor Emeritus of Pastoral Counseling
Union Theological Seminary in Virginia

Acknowledgments

I am sincerely grateful to the team of professionals at Westminster/John Knox Press. Alexa Smith, during her tenure there as editor, shepherded me for three years in the writing of this book. Editor Harold Twiss helped me complete the project.

Several readers shared keen insight that also shaped the book. For those extra miles I am indebted to Morris Berman, Joyce Deaton, Marty Settle, and Sally Mixon Thomas (my wife). To my utter amazement and delight, I discovered what a genius Sally is at copyediting.

I deeply appreciate the support of colleagues in the National Association of Bodyworkers in Religious Service, many of whom allowed inclusion of references to their work. For their encouraging words and prayers I thank Eleanor DelBene, Julie Dennison, Ellen Donovan, Charlotte Kerr, Dallas Landrum, Keith Raske, and Mary Ann Wamhoff.

I am grateful to Arne Jessen, Executive Director of the College of Chaplains, for supporting my efforts to create in the college a specialty group on touch. At the 1990 convention in Nashville, Arne said the college needed a resource on this subject. I shared his idea at the Westminster/John Knox book display table. The woman staffing the table, Alexa Smith, put the ball back in my court.

This serendipitous beginning characterized the project throughout. Frequently, just the right documents would appear on my desk at just the right time. Experiencing a larger creative process was inspiring, especially when it was necessary to engage gruesome material on touch from our all too human past. If this book moves us in any way out of that past to follow more faithfully the One who quells our compulsions and quickens our compassion, I am thankful, indeed.

Introduction

Upon arriving on the scene for parish ministry in the late 1960s, I soon experienced resistance to making pastoral calls—just as wise seminary professors had predicted. However, what surprised me was the way touch figured in the problem. I would become especially uncomfortable, to the point of embarrassment at times, whenever a person wanted to hold hands as we prayed. In the 1970s any person or activity called "touchy-feely" I avoided like the plague (and still do for that matter). The issues raised by touch—intimacy, sexuality, power, to name a few—I did not want to face. I would protect myself from affectionate feelings by turning a hug into a kind of backslapping, joking gesture. Though I have come to appreciate the importance of healthy resistance to touch, an awkward uneasiness with touch unconsciously affected my behavior in those days.

Now I lead workshops in touch and healing ministry for congregations, colleges, and various professional groups and have become a bodywork therapist. The event that led me in this direction was a professional massage I received in Switzerland in 1983. During the experience I sensed that I was sloughing off longstanding hang-ups about human touch. Not only was I putting aside the sexualized stereotype I associated with professional touchers, I was learning about a more direct way of expressing the treasures of the heart: healing energies, empathy, joy, delight, compassion. I was to spend years developing the connection between heart and hand, but the initial steps on this journey began there in Davos.

Back home, I did not have any difficulty in persuading Sally, my wife, to learn massage with me. Within a year I had graduated from a massage school. Sally and I started teaching our friends. I noticed an increase in body awareness, which in turn sharpened my pastoral skills as a hospital chaplain. I began teaching the importance of touch to hospital staff and to colleagues in chaplaincy. Discovering other clergy who had become professional bodyworkers, I formed the National Association of Bodyworkers in Religious Service (NABRS).[1]

After twelve years in hospital chaplaincy, I decided to attend directly to the new shaping of my vocation. Feeling a need to learn from cultures in which ancient healing arts of touch are still practiced, I took a two-month sabbatical to study various forms of bodywork in China and Hawaii. Three years later I took another leave to study Thai bodywork, which has been handed down for generations by Buddhist monks and is now taught at the Wat Po Temple in Bangkok and at a school in Chiang Mai.

Simple human touch has profoundly enriched my life and broadened my theology of pastoral care. It has given me the experience I needed to understand healing ministry more thoroughly. At the same time, "hands-on" experience has made me aware of glaring omissions in my training and practice of ministry. In seminary the New Testament record of Jesus' touching was largely ignored. In mainline churches I have attended, healing services with laying on of hands never occurred. It is ironic that a religion espousing faith in an embodied God is expressed in a church and a culture that have forgotten the body's language. I am convinced that the lessons we learn through touch can move us beyond our mind/body split—"the illness that we are"[2]—and reconnect us to the wholeness God creates and calls us to be.

Remembering Healing Touch

We start recovering from our splitness and begin to live in wholeness when we as Christians begin taking seriously the example set by our leader. Touch was an integral part of Jesus' compassion for others. To imagine his life and work without the use of touch is impossible.

Yet today we fear that touch may be misunderstood, manipulative, sexual, controlling, a disrupter of the psychological dynamics of transference in counseling, or a downright superstitious gesture in worship. Indeed, touch can be all these things.

Still, these problems cannot obscure all those stories about Jesus with outstretched hand, found on practically every page of the Gospels. Nor do they change the fact that he called us to continue both his teaching and healing ministry. I have written this book to help us remember touch as part of Christian healing ministry and to recall why we need to reclaim it.

What is healing touch, and what is it not? Healing touch is not "faith healing" or "faith cure." The final test of healing touch is not that it fixes or repairs something physically damaged. It is not "touch therapy" or a bodywork skill such as massage. Neither is it a new pastoral tool or a liturgical fad. It is not something we add to our repertoire or "get certified in." While healing touch may be experienced in these and many other ways, it is certainly not confined to or owned by one tradition or profession.

Rather, healing touch, as discussed in this book, refers to an important way of sharing compassion, primarily in three areas of experience:

1. Informal caring relationships among friends, family, and church groups.
2. Formal professional settings, including relationships between clergy, pastoral counselors, educators, bodyworkers, other therapists and those they serve.
3. Worship.

More specifically, healing touch is understood as an expression of a potential built into every one of us. I call this God-given capacity "heart/hand coordination" (see chapter 3). It develops naturally. We exercise heart/hand coordination whenever we communicate through touch the compassion we feel toward those receiving our care. In other words, a healing touch is basically part of our love and compassion for one another, and, as such, it facilitates healing ministry in many ways.

Remembering healing touch is a process of reconnecting with potentials in our body selves. Any healing touch emerges out of the capacity for heart/hand coordination we already have. This kind of remembering would be similar to reclaiming other behaviors that throughout the years have been forgotten, neglected, or overgrown by unhealthy habits. Take, for example, the simple act of breathing. It often becomes a shallow, constricted action for those under constant stress. Inhaling and exhaling more efficiently can be learned from ancient yogic breathing practices. Or look at the way we sit, stand, and carry things. We often prove in these actions that we have, indeed, forgotten the body's language. Instruction in correct body mechanics often draws from the postures taught for centuries in China through the art of tai chi. Such training, ancient or modern, does not teach us anything we do not already know. The exercises merely help us remember in these instances what our lungs, legs, and backs are naturally made to do and, furthermore, enjoy doing.

The same is true with touch. When awakening to our capacity for healing touch, we experience two things simultaneously. One is release (and relief) from meanings and behaviors that associate touch mainly with intentions to control. The other experience is the actual realignment of touch with the center of heartfelt compassion. Release from compulsions to control and realignment with reserves of compassion both feel good, enabling us to live more fully. Basically, in reclaiming healing touch, we are remembering how good and whole it feels when heart, hand, and healing process are coordinated.

This is why we want to remember and reclaim healing touch. It provides a form for celebrating the goodness and wholeness God creates and calls us to be. To live out of these wellsprings is a great joy. When touch emerges from the depths of our integrity in this manner it serves as a conduit, pouring compassionate energies where they are most needed: better communication between spouses, more wholesome parent–child relationships, healthier rituals in worship, more effective pastoral care, and clearer messages of inclusion to those who have begun to think of themselves as untouchables. Any one of these fruits of healing touch would be reason enough to reclaim it. Yet none is so basic a motivation as the sheer inner joy, goodness, and wholeness that healing touch calls forth in the giver.

Does this mean that healing touch is essentially a selfish act? No, our inner lives—our souls—are deeply connected with our bodies, their actions and experiences. Traditionally, we analyze inner motives to explain or change outer behavior. We do not often scrutinize physical activity as a means for shaping the inner life. Yet when Jesus said, "Do this in remembrance of me," he assumed, I imagine, that his followers' actions would play a part in keeping alive their connection with him in their hearts. Islam teaches that ordered movement of the body polishes the mirror of the soul. "Satan is said to lament whenever two Muslims shake hands. This simple physical contact between two human creatures is a token of the unity which Satan . . . wishes to shatter."[3] One of the reasons pastoral psychologist Paul W. Pruyser recommends that clergy apply more robust blessing with the hands is precisely the good it does for the clergy's own inner life. "Movements and gestures are psychodynamically so . . . closely interwoven with emotions that attempts at performing the proper motion are very likely to stimulate the corresponding emotion also."[4]

The practice of giving and receiving healing touch—as well as witnessing it, for example, in liturgy—prompts the heart's compassion and gives it a form to be of service in healing processes. In this manner, reclaiming healing touch moves us between action and reflection to learn from the interplay of body and soul. Theologian Jürgen Moltmann aptly summarizes what we might call the educative principle that enables us to remember healing touch. "The body 'informs' its soul just as strongly as the soul 'informs' its body."[5]

Proceeding with Caution

We need to be quite humble about touch. What we think we can do with this gesture, given its proper intentions, expectations, and settings, may not be as great as we anticipated and may be better accomplished through other means. Then again, we may be able to use touch intentionally for a variety of health purposes we have never thought about in the past. At present the Touch Research Institute (directed by Tiffany M. Field) of the Department of Pediatrics at the University of Miami School of Medicine is studying the effects of touch on several illnesses, including its capacity to modify body image and eating disorders in adolescents and reduce pain in arthritic patients. The point is that touch is so multifaceted it has the capacity both to bring us home to our human limits and to surprise us with our possibilities.

If only reaching out to touch someone were as uncomplicated as the telephone commercial would have us imagine! Touch, in league with gravity, is the primary sense that connects us to all physical reality. Furthermore, fueled by our feelings and intentions, touch connects us soul to soul—playfully, sensually, spiritually. The people with whom I was traveling in Central America in 1987 agreed that our conversion to peacemaking in that region came about primarily from holding the hands of homeless children. So healing touch is not just a fad for rich North Americans or a technique for counselors. It can be provided by a child, and it carries the fruits of compassion to the ends of the earth.

On the other hand, we need constant reminders of how touch is misused (see chapter 2). Touch can become the behavior around which we pack our fears and compulsions. I have heard these feelings expressed many times by workshop participants telling their "touch histories."

Yet the capacity of touch to connect us to the mystery and goodness of life, evoking trust and wonder, seems to be its most fundamental role. I am hearing more often now of people moving away from fearfulness to wholesome attitudes and behaviors related to human touch. In such cases there is a recurring factor. These individuals recall experiences that enabled them to reclaim their bodies as part of a created order God said was good. Embracing God-given goodness generates energy at the core to move from no-touch (or anti-touch) attitudes to a more Christlike style that is freer to give and receive healing touch. We are in a much more healthy frame of mind when we proceed and lead others in this humble spirit.

What to Expect

As noted previously, the instances of healing touch discussed in this book occur in three main areas—caring relationships, professional settings, and worship. To encourage healing touch in these areas is to help recover the church's forgotten language. Nevertheless, such reclamation challenges the habits of recent centuries in Christian nurture and pastoral care.

Therefore, Part 1 of this book seeks to clarify basic assumptions, historical realities, and central concepts. Chapter 1 discusses biblical and scientific reasons for concluding that God creates and calls us to use healing touch for developing healthy personalities and relationships. Chapter 2 tells the story of how we came to fear and misuse touch in Western religion and culture; unless we confront this sad chapter in our historical and personal experience, we cannot reclaim healing touch with integrity. Chapter 3 provides a basic vocabulary for ongoing discussion of touch—specifically, the concepts of health and wholeness, healing process, and heart/hand coordination.

Part 2 looks at practical aspects of touch by using case studies from pastoral care and worship. Chapter 4 examines intention, the most important factor in touch behavior. Chapter 5 discusses the expectations of givers and receivers of touch in various settings and provides guidelines on how to assess and make referrals to modern professional bodyworkers. Chapter 6 focuses on worship as a setting for healing touch: the intention of the act, healthy expectations of receivers, and practical considerations for including this gesture in liturgy.

I hope the book will help you accomplish the following six objectives:

1. Identify causes of unhealthy touch behavior, including the mind/body split.
2. Describe healthy touch and healthy no-touch behavior.
3. Outline experiences of recovery (such as from loss or illness) in terms of the healing process and describe how touch facilitates this process.
4. Demonstrate appropriate use of touch in pastoral care episodes.
5. Make proper referrals to bodywork professionals.
6. Apply sound principles of touch in designing and leading liturgies appropriate to healing ministry.

In an age that habitually attempts to think its way into heaven or make headway for the kingdom on earth, it will feel strange to reclaim a more organic but direct way. Nevertheless, a fuller understanding of Jesus and Christian ministry may come about only as we learn to speak the church's forgotten language of touch. Doing so may surprise us, not because it demands something heavy and complicated but precisely because it seems so light and simple.

Recall the story of Peter and John approached by the lame man outside the temple (Acts 3:1–16). They were caught unawares. Apparently, the custom was to give money to the sick one, but they had no money. They could only extend their hands in the name of Christ. I'm sure Peter and John were just as amazed as the crowd at what happened after that.

The purpose of healing touch is not to astound medical experts by miraculous feats or to control any other outcome. The point is simply to act in cooperation with the one who sent us out. For this task we do not need "silver or gold" or even touch therapy credentials. The authority we need is already head of the church. Christ calls us to preach *and* reach out to be part of the healing.

What more do we need? Well, to keep our wits about us will help. I hope this book enables us to be both realistic and creative in our hands-on endeavors. Allow touch to arise out of faith and joy in the good gift of God's presence in all creation. There we will find the passion that, when shared with others, becomes *com*passion. In doing so we become co-creators with God and followers of Christ (Matt. 10:1). And our works of faith become psalms of praise as of old.

> You anoint my head with oil;
>   my cup overflows.
> Surely goodness and mercy
>   shall follow me
> all the days of my life.
>   (Psalm 23:5–6)

PART 1

Touch in Western Healing Traditions

CHAPTER 1

Called and
Created to Touch

Healing touch: Jesus' ministry featured it. Similarly, early Christians, in their homes and rituals, frequently used it. Somewhere along the way we lost it. We passed it on to clergy, then to medical professionals, and even to the fringe of faith healers and others who exploit the gullible. In so doing we unwittingly forfeited a heartfelt way of expressing Christian faith.

We did not realize the extent to which hearts are linked with hands in communicating compassion. A "hands-off" Christianity splits us from our bodies and feelings. When compassion does not flow through us, refreshing us in the very act of obedience, we block spiritual energy. If it backs up into our heads, Christianity becomes an intellectual dilemma or a political strategy. Joy wanes. At worst, the energy churns chaotically and fuels abusive behaviors.

What will it take to reclaim healing touch? Changes in touch behaviors and attitudes toward the body are needed, of course. More important, we must seek a deeper understanding of healing and the role of touch in the commission to heal. Let's first talk briefly about healing. Later, in chapter 3, we will explore more thoroughly this fundamentally important subject.

Long ago, Christians expected physical cures to accompany the laying on of hands in baptism, communion, and special services for the sick. Just as the ancient Greeks left offerings to their healing god, Asclepius, in appreciation for recoveries they attributed to his "divine touch," so the early Christians pointed to cures in their midst as evidence of Jesus' healing presence.

These old records are intriguing. I must confess, however, that throughout many years of working in nursing homes, hospitals, and rehabilitation centers, giving and receiving thousands of hours of professional bodywork, and attending several healing services, I have never witnessed or experienced the instantaneous cures historically attributed to healing touch.

Undoubtedly, such miracles occurred in the past and still do, if we are to believe, for example, the carefully documented evidence from the shrine in Lourdes, France. But even at this special place, physical cure is the exception, not the rule. What does happen more commonly is a "tremendous transformation of faith"[1] that enables people to live more fully regardless of the outcome of their physical illness.

If we imagine a similar experience for the early Christians, we may be closer to the truth. Certainly they celebrated cures of various ailments as evidence of God's presence in Christ among them. Even Augustine of Hippo (A.D. 354–430), skeptical as he was about such phenomena, began in his later years to pay closer attention to these dramatic instances, some of which happened before his very eyes. But these special cases rarely became the sole data upon which Christians based their understanding of healing.

In addition to (and perhaps more important than) physical cure, healing also meant the power to decide for sexual abstinence (as in Augustine's case), to live in an ascetic or monastic community, or to accept martyrdom. In short, healing had to do with surrendering to the powerful love of God for the radical changing of one's life.

For early Christians, whose living conditions were as severe as in any third-world country today, sickness represented the ever-present specter of death. In that context, healing touch functioned as much to encourage faith in Christ's victory over death and hope in his imminent return as it did to channel healing energies for specific ills. As a result of healing touch, the first Christians expected "not simply bodily healing but a deeper wholeness: strength, forgiveness of sins, vivification, protection of body, mind, and spirit."[2] Thus, from the beginning, healing touch was not essentially a private moment but was shaped by the church's efforts to encourage wholeness and community in the midst of life's harsh realities.

In reclaiming healing touch today, we need to keep in mind these larger contexts of healing process. The "miracles" of touch are real, but they are by no means restricted to the physical domain without regard for the network of relationships to which the person belongs.

For example, a woman became depressed after her husband was sent to the Gulf War. Her stomach remained in knots even after he returned. It made her constipated and emotionally volatile. She said, "I go around feeling I'm about to cry."

One day a visiting friend put an arm around her, resting her hand on the tense abdomen. The friend said, "Imagine what the knot looks like. Now picture the grace of God coming down like a blanket covering and dissolving it."

After the friend left, the woman began talking aloud to God in a conversational manner that her friend seemed to have opened up for her. "There's so much suffering," she lamented. "The war, the homeless, pain everywhere you look." She listed all the things that depressed her. As she prepared to conclude the talk, she threw one parting shot at God. "And most of all, I'm tired of resenting you." That did it. Sobs shook her body. Tears washed her soul.

"It was like God was practically standing on top of me, untying the knot in my stomach, " she said.

In a week the knot disappeared, but more profoundly a healing process had begun. The woman came to a much clearer understanding of her depression. Her friend had helped open up life-giving channels that would greatly enrich her walk with God.

Notice the expanded meanings we have already begun to associate with the phrase "healing touch." We are not talking about repairing, curing, or easing physical pain. The woman's friend touched a knotted stomach but also a heavy heart. Touch helped communicate a compassion that brought the woman into a deeper healing process involving her relationship with God and her husband, not to mention her stomach.

Touch therapies today sometimes miss subtleties of the larger healing process. Instead, they often aim to assuage the symptom or achieve a cure. It is certainly not wrong to want someone's effective touch to ease a headache or a backache. Indeed, when one's faith is tested by physical or emotional trials, a soothing touch that eases pain can also be a faith strengthener. We deeply appreciate these acts of kindness. Nonetheless, as useful as these services may be, they—as anything else (pills, for example)—can become the focal point. When that happens, we begin looking more toward the cure (or curer) than to the one who makes both curing and healing possible.

Doing this is an ancient temptation. In the fourth century the monk Macarius intentionally wore himself out carrying heavy loads across the sand so he would have no energy left to go to Rome and show off his gift for curing the sick.[3] In A.D 355 the great theologian Athanasius wrote, "We must not boast of . . . the healing of diseases. . . . To work miracles is not ours; that is the Saviour's work."[4] Athanasius reminded his hearers of Jesus' teaching: "Do not rejoice at this, that the spirits submit to you, but rejoice that your names are written in heaven" (Luke 10:20).

Again, let's not belittle the immediate good that human touch can accomplish. Massage, for example, can cure many ills caused by muscle tension, such as headaches, insomnia, and restricted range of motion. However, these results are not miracles. What indicates that a deeper healing is occurring are comments during or after massage such as these:

"This is the unconditional love I never felt as a child but always wanted."
"My body's a puzzle being put back together."
"I'm aware of parts I'm usually unaware of and how they are connected to a whole."
"I felt you accepting my foot, which is so ugly to me. It made me think of Jesus washing the disciples' feet."

One person using massage therapy to recover from the ongoing emotional scars of childhood sexual abuse said, "With this touch I feel safe again."

Such benefits can never be engineered. Rather, they come out of the person's faith, hope, and love mixed with God's grace and facilitated by compassionate touch. In other words, they are the fruit of a healing process directed by God.

The healing process, which will be explored more fully in chapter 3, contains significant moments that lead to greater health, as conceived in the biblical notion of shalom. Such wholeness refers to integrity in the individual (of body, mind, and soul) as well as in community (of relationships to God, one another, and the earth). Indeed, health in the Bible is understood as a function of the quality of communal relationship. Since touch is a community builder, it figures prominently in healing processes directed toward shalom. To cooperate with that healing through touch is a great joy and privilege. As a client once told me, "God and my body are the healers. Your hands are just the tutors."

There is much to be said on behalf of the tutorial nature of healing touch. It is the homework that enriches relationships between husband and wife, parents and children. It encourages a family's communication and sense of play. It enables spiritual friendships to mature. It brings hospital chaplains and hospice volunteers closer to those they serve. In the form of intentional touch therapies, healing touch can improve the lives of those who feel estranged as a result of abuse, addiction, or depression. In worship, touch deepens the integrity of rituals of healing. Touch is healing when it serves, in these and many other ways, the purposes of larger healing processes.

Can Christians in families, churches, and seminaries learn once again to touch compassionately? Can congregations once again coordinate heart and hand in liturgies for healing? Maybe, if we are not continually fearful of the body. Maybe, if we are sure such a project is not a New Age fad. Maybe, if we know we won't be mistaken for charlatans or lechers. However, we can answer a definite "yes" if we are convinced that touch is an essential part of healing ministry; "yes" if we are certain healing touch is one of the gifts of the Spirit entrusted to the community of faith.

To support that "yes" we need the best biblical and scientific evidence we can find. In an age grown suspicious from abuse of power, we want to be as clear as possible about the foundations of our behavior. Let us take a closer look at how we have been called and created to use healing touch.

Authority and Method

The authority of Christian faith has always been mediated in a twofold manner: through the symbols and standards of the church (such as scripture, sacraments, and creeds) and through the Spirit's presence in the context of human life (nature and individual and communal experience, for example). Obviously, these two modes are inextricably related. But the church's methods of using authority have not always held these two poles in balance.

Scholasticism in the Middle Ages argued that all Christian belief should be based on the authority of the church. Reformers renounced this approach in order to anchor authority in the Bible. However, the reformers' liberation from ecclesiastical chains depended so heavily on *sola scriptura* that the Bible became another external authority and thus another instrument of human pride.

Increasing reliance on the Bible meant that the other mode of revelation—the "book of the natural world"—would be discounted. Thomas Berry, head of New York's Center for Religious Research, says "in the sixteenth century . . . the whole emphasis shifted over to biblical texts. That essentially weakened our sense of the natural world as our primary revelatory experience . . . much of which was based on the first chapter of Saint Paul's epistle to the Romans, in which he mentions that we come to know the divine world from the phenomenal world."[5] Thus the idea that one might find valuable resources for theology in nature and human experience is an ancient one. Only recently, after centuries of neglect, is it being articulated once again in modern thought by liberal and creation-centered theologians.

In our approach, we reclaim the book of the natural world as we know it through the body. It may seem strange to pay attention to anatomical and anthropological details to sharpen our theological understanding. But we need only to stop and remember that our Christian heritage points us to a God who becomes flesh, who dwells within and among us, and who bodily resurrects us into the very life of God. We pay attention to this God because of the way the divine presence registers itself in the body (Deut. 30:11–14; Matt. 11:2–6). Early Christians did not hesitate to ground the source of their authority for Gospel truth in both received traditions and in their sensory experience. They spoke of "what was from the beginning, what we have heard, what we have seen with our eyes, what we have looked at and touched with our hands, concerning the word of life" (1 John 1:1).

Thus the question of authority in discussions of healing touch will always refer both to Jesus *and* to our bodily experience. These two sources may be separated for purposes of discussion only. In reality, they are inseparable. We cannot speak authoritatively about either one without eventually referring to the other. And that is our method.

In this method, we examine the truth about Jesus' healing work, especially his characteristic expression of compassion through touch, from the point of view of what we know and experience of the healing process and of the body's touch capacities and behaviors. This method brings a deeper understanding of Jesus himself and points toward directions in faith and practice that are more consistent with his calling to preach *and* heal. Its integrity depends on how Jesus and the body are interpreted. In considering Jesus, the interpretive (hermeneutical) task has to do with the way biblical material is chosen and meaning is translated. This is no small task, but it pales in comparison to interpreting the body.

Interpreting the body requires paying close attention not only to personal experience but also to the influence of cultural and historical settings on one's perception of the body. During the early seventeenth century, scientists were so enamored of the powers of the mind they had little regard for the body. In 1619, French philosopher René Descartes had an experience from which he concluded, "I saw that I could conceive that I had no body and . . . that I was a substance whose whole essence or nature was only to think and which to exist has no need of space or any material thing."[6] Today, thought processes such as memory, intuition, insight, and creativity are no longer studied solely as functions of the mind. Rather, they are understood by examining the whole body's chemistry, kinesthetics, and other aspects.

In reality there may be as many interpretations of the body as there are people. However, at least three models of the person and nature will serve us well as interpretive frameworks. These models have been suggested by philosopher Renee Weber in her essay "Philosophers on Touch."[7]

The *physical* model relates to "contact" definitions of touch. It fits most Anglo-American thought and scientific tradition inherited from Descartes and Hume. From this viewpoint, touch is perceived as a stimulus-response phenomenon, as studied by B. F. Skinner and others.

The *developmental* model corresponds to definitions of touch as communication. It moves beyond the first model, which Martin Buber would label an "I–It" approach, to what Buber calls "I–Thou" relationships. This second model draws from existentialist thinking on human subjectivity, consciousness, and personhood. Touch, from this perspective, conveys meaning.

The *energetic* model correlates with definitions of touch as laying on of hands. Its basic concept is energy, common to Eastern religions. As persons become capable of tuning in to the larger energy fields of which they are a part, they may facilitate order and harmony for others in many ways, including touch. In this model touch becomes therapeutic, in a sense reaching back to Plato's ideal of caring *with* hands as well as *through* them, a task requiring ego to be both intentional and non-attached.

Since human experience is vastly richer than what is contained in any single model, no model is absolutely authoritative in and of itself or even in combination with others. It is true that broader perception of the body is afforded in approaches that include more than one model. However, searching for the ultimate, syncretistic paradigm of the body is surely as fruitless as rigidly defending any one traditional model.[8]

In this battle of the paradigms, the life, death, and resurrection of Jesus will always stand as additional experiential reality that is not fully contained in any model. As a result, Jesus' example transcends the others as a model of the person and nature. In another sense, his reality cannot be understood except in terms of these (or other) models, which contain so much of the bodily realities Jesus shares with us all. Here we encounter the truth, as earlier stated, that the two sources of authority used in our method—Jesus and bodily context—are inextricably related. We will take a closer look at each of them.

Biblical Sources

Judaism located the power to both heal and destroy with Yahweh (Deut. 32:39). Thus sickness, such as leprosy, was viewed as God's punishment for sin. Since only God could make holy what was unclean, elaborate rituals of purification occupied the Levitic priesthood. Taboos against touching the unclean were meticulously spelled out (Lev. 22:4–8).

In non-Jewish cultures both predating and contemporaneous with Judaism, rituals for childbirth, tending to the sick, and burying the dead were frequently carried out by those who acknowledged other forces at work, such as demons, in healing and disease. The Levites, however, made sure there was no room for competition with Yahweh. Any necromancers, sorcerers, witches, augurers, mediums, or wizards were to be stoned to death (Lev. 20:27). Judaism grew to be remarkably devoid of anyone designated as healer. In fact, the only reference in the Old Testament to someone consulting a physician is King Asa, and his action was viewed as betrayal: "Even in his disease he did not seek the LORD, but sought help from physicians" (2 Chron. 16:12). Since Jesus touched the unclean and exorcised demons, we can understand why the Talmud states that the reason for Jesus' crucifixion was sorcery.[9]

Healing Traditions

If Jesus was not a sorcerer, what tradition informed the path of the healer that he took? In Judaism only hints of healing

11

remained: a few healing stories (1 Kings 17:17–23; 2 Kings 4:18–37; 5:1–14), some psalms (41, 116, 147), passages in Isaiah (35:5–6; 61:1–3), and especially Job, which challenged the entire system of thought that linked sickness with sin.[10] Apparently, this important but minor prophetic theme did not escape Jesus' study of scripture. He chose Isaiah 61:1–2 as the basic description of his mission (Luke 4:18–19). Nonetheless, in Judaism the function of traditional healers had practically disappeared. Our search for background to Jesus' ministry must include non-Jewish sources.

In *Healing and Christianity,* Morton Kelsey suggests that shamanic traditions offer the most likely source of inspiration.[11] Since Jesus mediates between physical and spiritual realities and thereby attends to disease and healing, he steps into the shaman's role. Classical historians Emma J. and Ludwig Edelstein see the Greek healing god Asclepius as the archetype of the physician that Jesus embodied.[12] Indeed, the resemblance was so keen in the popular mind for centuries that the early church made Asclepius a chief target of attack in order to distinguish him from Jesus. Monica Sjoo and Barbara Mor, researching prehistorical religions, find that the first healers and shamans were women using their knowledge of biological cycles, midwifery, herbs, and spirituality. Since later patriarchal religions took over over these functions, Jesus, in their estimation, "acts out a female role."[13]

While none of these theories totally explains the path Jesus took, they all carry grains of truth. Especially are we more likely to associate Jesus with these non-Jewish sources when we take note of his mothering/touching/healing activity. He called his disciples children or friends, comforted them in their fears with his touch, washed their feet, fed them (of his own "body"), and cooked them breakfast. He welcomed and held children, touched sick bodies across social taboos, and had a remarkable relationship with women, given the standards of his day. He demonstrated the kind of mutuality in relationship to the feminine within himself and others that contrasts starkly with his culture (and, we might add, offers a much-needed antidote to modern-day psyches compelled to control).

However, the differences between Jesus and non-Jewish healing traditions are as significant as the similarities. Perhaps the main difference concerns the role of altered states of consciousness. The shaman's drum, Asclepius's dreams, and the witch's drugs aided traditional healing work, opening consciousness to larger psychic reserves. Though spiritual and psychological factors also played an important part in Jesus' approach, his style of integrating body and soul did not include the accouterments of traditional healers. He used no elaborate rituals, no sacred temples, and no secret potions. If anything characterized his healing, it would be his words and his healing touch.

The first church historian, the author of Acts, was decidedly less curious than we about precedents on which Jesus might have patterned his work. In that account, Jesus' work was part of and consistent with Jewish covenant keeping. The summary simply states that "he went about doing good and healing" (Acts 10:38). This language is characteristic of those who attend faithfully to relationships, who do the things necessary to keep families and communities thriving and healthy. The Hebrew idea is *hesed,* translated as steadfast love, faithfulness, kindness, and goodness. "*Hesed* . . . is . . . an act of goodness, but it is one that can be expected, since it takes place within the context of a covenant of intimate fellowship." [14] Another Hebrew word for "good"—*tov*—is used in a similar manner. When God creates the world and calls it *tov* (Gen. 1:10), the goodness serves to confirm God's pleasure in relation to the creation. [15]

So by doing good and healing, Jesus savors the experience of human life and enriches it with acts of goodness and kindness that delight body and soul and bear fruit that builds community. Deeds of *hesed* are not showy or dramatic. They may even go unnoticed and to some extent are even expected. But they are never insignificant. Jesus' stories of the good and faithful servants (Matt. 25:14–23) and the good Samaritan (Luke 10:29–37) illustrate the *hesed* he embodied.

Whatever healing tradition Jesus resembled, he certainly practiced the good news he preached in terms of covenant-keeping behavior. We will now look at his ministry from the point of view of touch, the goodness it expressed, and the healing it facilitated.

New Testament Sources

Jesus' healing ministry occupies one fifth of the Gospel accounts.[16] His "most common means of healing was by speaking words and touching the sick person with his hand."[17] When the Gospel writers describe Jesus' ministry among the multitudes, they picture him touching those who come to him for healing (Mark 6:5; Luke 4:40).

Likewise, the writers remember the crowds seeking out Jesus for his touch (Mark 10:13). In Bethsaida, people brought a blind man to Jesus and "begged him to touch him" (Mark 8:22).

Of forty-one references to Jesus' healing ministry in the Gospels, twenty-two are stories of healing work with an individual.[18] Of these specific cases, fourteen (64 percent) involve touch along with Jesus' words of comfort and exhortation. Typical of these stories is Mark's account of a leper who comes to Jesus. "Moved with pity, Jesus stretched out his hand and touched him, and said to him, '. . . Be made clean!'" (Mark 1:41). Notice how touch originates in Jesus' deep feelings of compassion. His story of the good Samaritan contains these same dynamics (Luke 10:33–34). In chapters 3 and 4 we will discuss in more detail this coordination of heart and hand in healing touch.

Jesus commissioned the disciples to carry out his ministry (Matt. 10:5–8; Mark 6:7–13; Luke 9:1–6). Their healing work also included touch. Peter, for example, confronted by a lame man, "took him by the right hand and raised him up" (Acts 3:7). In *And You Visited Me: Sacramental Ministry to the Sick and the Dying,* an excellent history of the ritual aspects of healing touch, Charles W. Gusmer concludes that "in the gospels and Acts, the laying on of hands (touching) is the healing gesture par excellence."[19]

Paul calls the results of their healing ministries "miracles" (Gal. 3:5) and "signs and wonders" (Rom. 15:19; 2 Cor. 12:12). These words, the same used to describe Jesus' healing works, assured the readers that the events ultimately signaled the active presence of God in their midst. Since the action engaged people with physical, mental, and moral problems, Paul drew both from clinical vocabulary ("to cure," "restore," "heal") and from theological language ("to preserve," "save"). With its source in God's power and love, healing ministry was called "gifts" of the Holy Spirit (1 Cor. 12:9, 28–30).

The church community reached out to heal in obedience to their master. Jesus had modeled a ministry of healing touch and had commissioned his followers to go and do likewise. They obeyed.

To be sure, curing and healing occurred in a variety of ways: through prayer, the faith of friends, and sacraments, among others. Some scholars take note of two different kinds of healing gestures mentioned in the New Testament—namely, "touch" and "laying on of hands."[20] Others study the way oil ("chrism") is associated with healing touch.[21] In the New Testament only two instances are recorded of the religious use of oil with the sick—by the disciples (Mark 6:13) and by church leaders (James 5:14–15). Given the rich symbolism associated with oil in biblical times and Jesus' openness to the use of substances in gestures of healing (Luke 10:33–34; John 9:6–7) and of kindness (Matt. 26:6–12), it is likely that he would have used oil on occasion. However, there is no record of his doing so. Nor do we find in scripture that Jesus mandates the use of oil or any specific technique, including touch, for acts of healing. The efficacy of healing ministry was never dependent on the presence or absence of touch or other means. The importance of touch lay not in its powers, as if it were inherently magic. Rather, its worth obtained from the fact that it was so thoroughly built into healing ministry from the start.

Why did Jesus use touch in healing? We cannot be certain. Just as he used everyday images in parables and took bread and wine at the Last Supper, so he chose a simple and familiar means of expressing compassion in healing.

In light of this biblical record, there can be no doubt that we are encouraged to offer healing touch by the example Jesus sets before us. Although Paul's list of the Spirit's gifts indicates that some persons may have attended to healing as a calling (1 Cor. 12:4–11), the gift of healing was never considered to be owned by any particular group. Indeed, the idea that special powers of the laying on of hands could be controlled as so much personal property was severely nipped in the bud (Acts 8:14–24). Rather, the gift is freely given to the whole community of faith. None of the disciples as far as we know was trained in health care. Yet all were sent out to preach *and* heal. The classic text for the church's healing ministry, James 5:14–16, reveals that extending a healing hand was a responsibility felt by the total community of faith.

This gracious pouring out of the gift of healing, this quickening among the total body of Christ, demonstrates that what we have been called to do is within our capabilities. God has already prepared us for the task to which Jesus commissions us. We find evidence for this conviction in the authority of the body itself.

The Body's Sources

While the initial authority is Jesus, whose commission for healing ministry the Bible clearly records, the source that corroborates our sense of fitness for this ministry is found in the book of nature—specifically, the body. In the following discussion we will see how the body is made to give and receive touch for its very life, for its sense of self or wholeness, and for building relationships and community.

Touch for Life

One cannot live without touch. The same cannot be said of any of the other senses. Touch can be considered as one of the basics of survival, along with food, water, oxygen, rest and movement, elimination, and sensitivity to danger and pain. Studies of newborn animals and human beings show that neither can survive long without external stimulation. Animals stroked and held ("gentled") in their infancy not only survive but develop faster in every way than do those that remain isolated.[22] A 1988 *New York Times* article reported that premature infants massaged fifteen minutes daily "gained weight 47% faster than others who were left alone in their incubators, . . . showed signs that the nervous system was maturing more rapidly, . . . and were discharged from the hospital an average of six days earlier. Eight months later, the massaged infants did better in tests of mental and motor ability than the ones who were not massaged."[23]

The grim other side of the coin is a 1915 research project in orphanages where infant mortality within one year of admission was between 90 and 99 percent. The study showed that the deaths were caused by inadequate sensory stimulation.[24]

Our need for touch is more like our need for food. In fact, "the symptoms of sensory deprivation—retarded bone growth, failure to gain weight, poor muscular coordination, immunological weakness, general apathy—are strikingly similar to those of malnutrition."[25] Touch, like food, is life-giving.

Touch for Wholeness

Life that touch nurtures is more than skin deep. The skin and the central nervous system are intimately connected in the development of the whole person, the sense of one's self. The agency sparking the coordinated effort is touch.

Both the skin and the central nervous system develop from the same layer, ectoderm, in the early embryo. Recent studies of the developing fetus indicate that the brain's mapping of itself to correspond to certain areas of the body is not a process generated by the brain, as postulated in previous theories. Rather, the software necessary for the brain's organization is the skin. Its multiple sensory capacities feed data to the central nervous system without which the brain cannot develop properly. In reality, the skin can be understood as the "advancing boundary" of the central nervous system.[26]

Coordination between inner and outer neurological structure continues as we speak. The brain adjusts the size and shape of

areas (maps) on its convoluted surfaces according to the messages it receives from the skin. For example, the brain's map for
hands and fingers will increase to accommodate new sensory
input from repetitive activity such as massage. Researchers refer
to this experience-dependent characteristic as "brain plastic-
ity."[27] The phenomenon is important because it helps us appreciate the role of outer somatic experience in the formation
of inner aspects of the person. Such dynamics appear to be involved in the formation of a sense of wholeness, or self.

Sandra J. Weiss examined general psychological theories
that locate the origin of a person's sense of self in body awareness. More specifically, she wanted to know if the quality of
parental touch affected the child's body image. Working with a
group of eight- to ten-year-olds and their parents, Weiss con-
structed a series of activities monitored by observers trained to
identify four qualities of touch. She found a correlation between
healthy body image and the quality of the parents' touch.[28]

The lifelong connection between outer physical nurturance
and inner self emphasizes the importance of touch for ongoing
development of the individual's sense of integrity and wholeness. "We could even say that this role of the tactile senses in
establishing a fuller and fuller sense of self is their primary function."[29] Such facts help us see more clearly some of the issues
beneath the huge demand in our times for bodywork therapies.
Surely, for Western people these modern forms of the laying on
of hands are coloring the inner spaces of the psyche left blank
by mind/body splits from which we suffer in so many ways.

Lack of touch, or unwholesome touch, harms the integrity of
one's inner life. To examine the *intra*-personal damage, studies
such as Weiss's point us in the right direction—to the profound
ways in which sense of self is connected with the body. How
Western society developed a psyche split from the soma is the
subject of the next chapter. The point here is that the internal
psychic wounds that accompany less than adequate somatic
stimulation are deep, perpetuated by a cultural heritage that, in
turn, is an expression of wounded selves—a vicious cycle.

In light of the alliance between the skin and the central nervous system in developing the self, we might better understand how a misformed and angry self vents its rage on the evils it senses to have come from the exterior. The problem in locating evil in this superficial manner is that the mind is never convinced it has resolved the problem. Scapegoating only deflects the anger, leaving the angry one railing against externals as if the devil lived in the skin. The split between mind and body widens as the whole body, which the skin covers and represents, is considered evil. Conveniently, skin begins to serve as a sign of the enemy. Some sociologists see in these dynamics the origins of oppressive political and social systems.[30] Racial battles and prejudices are prime examples of how wounded selves allow skin—in this instance, its color—to organize their anger.

Such episodes, occurring all too frequently in human history, make us wonder whether our anatomical wiring predisposes us to self-destruct in a sort of knee-jerk defensiveness once the going gets rough on the outside. Is the human being capable of managing its inner/outer connections beyond the level of stimulus/response dictated by a purely physical model of the person and nature?

The Bible reveals a remarkable understanding of these somato-emotional dynamics. To cause Job the worst internal damage to the psyche, all God has to do is touch him, says Satan. "Skin for skin! . . . Stretch out your hand now and touch his bone and his flesh, and he will curse you to your face" (Job 2:4–5). But Job, covered with sores and sitting in ashes, maintains his inner life understood in terms of his relationship with God.

The story of Job, in a sense, tests the theory that one's inner wholeness is "experience-dependent." All human wisdom, represented by Job's counselors and his wife, believes it is. "Do you still persist in your integrity? Curse God, and die" (Job 2:9). There is more than an ounce of healthy anger in that counsel. But the purpose of the book of Job is to expose the ultimate superficiality of stimulus/response and to dramatize faith's capacity for embracing the opposites and contradictions of life deep in the soul. Out of such depths, Isaiah writes, "The wolf shall live with the lamb, the leopard shall lie down with the kid, the calf and the lion and the fatling together, and a little child shall lead them" (Isa. 11:6). Anyone who exercises these capacities brings healing and wholeness for the individual as well as for the entire community. "We accounted him stricken . . . by God [the superficial evaluation]. . . . But . . . upon him was the punishment that made us whole [the accurate depth analysis]" (Isa. 53:4–5).

Jesus understood these inner/outer dynamics. "Did not the one who made the outside make the inside also?" (Luke 11:40). Breaking through human veneer, he called the righteous elite "whitewashed tombs, which on the outside look beautiful, but inside . . . are full of the bones of the dead and of all kinds of filth" (Matt. 23:27). Jesus never stirred crowds to scapegoating frenzies by tying their hurts and fears to cultural externalities. Instead, he warned of those who "inwardly are ravenous wolves" (Matt. 7:15). One cannot identify such wolves by their skin but at best by their fruit. Even then, we are to love our enemies.

Like Job, Jesus experienced rejection. Designed, it seems, to inflict maximum inner suffering, the punishment was applied to his skin by beating, striking, scourging, slapping, pricking with reeds, puncturing by thorns, nails, and spear. Such treatment challenges the farthest reaches of the soul, to say the least. Rather than striking back, as did Peter with his sword, Jesus went beneath the surfaces of skin-for-skin behavior. We might say he transcended the stimulus/response mechanisms of a purely physical model of the body and thus gave us an example that is not bound to war with the enemy.

Nonetheless, given our neural construction, we learn much from the physical model to verify how healing touch can and does reach through the skin to facilitate restoration of the self. Family therapist Jeanne Zell reports what adult children of alcoholics gain from massage therapy: "Grounding. Connectedness. . . . Getting back in touch with their bodies. Increased self-confidence. Good deep release of feelings. Recalling memories. Widening the possibility of trust. . . . Intimacy. . . . Pure pleasure."[31] Positive nurturing through the skin does build both inner integrity and a healthy body politic. "Societies that are body-positive and convey this to children through touch and physical nurturance . . . are demonstrably much more coopera- tive, peaceful societies."[32]

How could we have a healthy sense of self if we have no family and neighbors grounding us in plenty of physical nurtur- ance? How could we love our neighbors as ourselves if we had no inner sense of self? And how could we love God without heart, soul, and might? The biblical way requires everything we have, inside and out. Fortunately, it is a life of wholeness for which we have been wondrously made and which healing touch can graciously restore.

Touch for Community

The life and wholeness that touch makes possible is commu- nity life. Otherwise, instead of being outfitted with cloth made to touch—our skin—we would have been created as isolated units. But, as it turned out, "we are formed not by abstract laws but by the intimacies of a wrestling match, where we struggle with universal forces until we begin to feel our individual forces grow in relation to them."[33] Touch often is called the mother of the senses, a metaphor reminding us that the anatomical foun- dation of our communal nature is our touchy skin.

In the development of the senses, touch is the first to become functional, appearing at six weeks in human embryos, when they are less than an inch long.[34] All other senses—hearing, smell, taste, and sight—are in actuality further refinements of "neural cells to particular kinds of touch: compression of air upon the ear drums, chemicals on the nasal membranes and taste buds, photons on the retina."[35] Though all senses decline with age, the need for touch seems to increase: "The first to ignite, touch is often the last to burn out. Long after our eyes betray us, our hands remain faithful to the world."[36]

Between birth and death touch creates the formative rela- tionships in which we live. Technically speaking, touch is one of a family of senses at work in establishing significant relationships. Two weeks after the sense of touch develops in the human embryo, the capacity of the inner ear to detect movement and the capacity of the muscles and tendons to sense movement are noticeable. In infancy all of these senses are involved in bonding through such a simple action as being picked up by a caring adult. By two years of age, the capacities of children to detect the quality of touch can be measured.[37]

Significant developmental and social processes show the importance of touch in communication, part of its community-building role. We are anatomically wired for communicating through touch. "Nerve fibers conducting tactile impulses are generally of larger size than those associated with other senses."[38] The brain reserves more area for receiving impulses from the hand than any other part of the body. In the most comprehensive study of touch behavior in everyday interaction, Jones and Yarbrough found that touch has more symbolic significance than previous research indicated. "A touch is ordinarily an undeniable message. . . . It is nearly impossible for a person to touch another and then claim no meaning was intended."[39]

What is communicated through touch? Jones and Yarbrough identified eighteen categories of meaning, twelve of which were unambiguous—to communicate support, appreciation, inclusion, sexual interest, affection, playfulness, compliance, attention getting, feeling, and ritual hellos and good-byes. Judging from this study, touch functions in its natural role as a facilitator of communication. "Verbal messages are interchangeable with tactile behavior."[40]

However, there is more to this study than these operational conclusions. One cannot read it without noticing the remarkably affirming, supportive, even playful nature of messages communicated through touch. The researchers said, "Tactile communication appears to be a form of approach behavior by its very nature. One cannot touch and, at the same time, be uninvolved with the other person."[41] Touch not only facilitates verbal communication, it also conveys a message of its own that brings the communicators into closer felt relationship.

If relationships can be built by touch, they can also be un-done by it. Negative effects of touch begin with one's inten-tions. Research with "therapeutic touch" shows that therapists' intentions affect the quality of touch as perceived by the re-ceiver.[42] In a study using massage therapy, the researcher found that negative expectations by the therapists strongly influenced clients to have negative experiences of the therapy sessions.[43]

Given the high marks our society assigns to status, domi-nance, power, and male privilege, it is no wonder that such val-ues are both intended and expected to be communicated through touch.[44] How this cultural conditioning paves the way for physically abusive behavior deserves serious consideration.

So powerful in forming community, touch breaks up rela-tionships when by its absence or misuse persons grow to feel "fearful or angry in every situation that normally arouses love or longing."[45] The National Institute of Child Health and Human Development concludes that unsatisfactory touch is among "the basic causes of a number of emotional disturbances, which include depressive and autistic behaviors, hyperactivity, sexual aberration, drug abuse, violence, and aggression."[46]

Pastors, caregivers, and churches can reverse these negative consequences by modeling healing touch. Frequently, in minis-tering to grieving families huddled in the corner of a hospital room, I have found that my touching their loved one gives fam-ily members unspoken permission to come to the bedside to express their compassion more effectively. Healing services whose liturgies contain a moment for laying on of hands func-tion in a similar manner for the whole faith community (see chapter 6). They open the door for a fuller experience of how we belong to the healing body of Christ.

Conclusion

In creating us for life, wholeness, and community, God de-signed touch to play a significant role. Jesus demonstrated the importance of touch as an example of the good deeds that facilitate the healing process and thus renew the bonds of covenant community. We are taught such roles both by Jesus and by our bodies, which God made fit for this purpose. We learn from the Bible and from various models of the body. Primarily they teach us that touch is necessary for life, that it nurtures integrity in individuals and communities and builds significant social bonds.

We noted how the absence or misuse of touch can kill, wound self-image, and break up relationships. Unfortunately, these negative consequences are to some extent the result of our failure to carry out the commission to heal.

Thus the next step in reclaiming healing touch is to take seriously our resistance to this commission. The resistance is composed of behaviors that ignore or misuse touch—behaviors that contribute to making our present cultural context a mind/body split.

CHAPTER 2

The Role of
Touch in the
Mind/Body Split

As chaplain in a physical reha-
bilitation hospital, I was often invited by patients to feel the
strength building up in their muscles. Indeed, through touch I
could sometimes detect progress within a period of just a few
weeks. One day a woman patient, delighted with the improvement in her arms, told me she wanted to find ways to exercise all her muscles, even though she was paralyzed from the
waist down. She asked me to bring her a picture of the body's
muscle groups.

After thumbing through all 1,216 pages of *Gray's Anatomy,* I
discovered there is not a single picture of the whole body in
that tome. It was unnerving to have to say, "Sorry! I can't find a
whole body right now."

I began to notice the many ways we treat people like Humpty
Dumpty—broken into pieces. Thinking of the body only as a
collection of parts, we literally lose sense of touching the whole
person. Touch that communicates with the whole person is
healing touch. It is also rare. As we shall see, the touch that is
far more common is *not* the kind that can ever put Humpty
Dumpty together again.

In a special to the *Utne Reader,* Andrew Kimbrell says, "Our
modern institutions of learning, work, food production, medicine, and even electronic amusement are . . . amputating our
intimate senses. . . . At the base of this crisis is a . . . complete
failure to understand the nature and meaning of the body itself."
He concludes, "We have declared war on our bodies."[1]

Body wars flare up when we allow one function to dominate
at the expense of others. Paul states, "The eye cannot say to the
hand, 'I have no need of you,' nor again the head to the feet, 'I

25

have no need of you'" (1 Cor. 12:21). But our society has decided that it is OK to do this. Collectively, we have given all the power to the mind. On our schools we carve KNOWLEDGE IS POWER. On our religion we put the label PEOPLE OF THE BOOK. The value of the senses is downplayed or ignored. Thus we hear, "Don't touch!" from our minds (or from the media or anyone who expresses prevailing taboos) and "Touch!" from our bodies. Or vice versa: the cultural mind-set wants us to reach out and touch someone, but the body intuitively recoils. Morris Berman, researcher of social change, says the history of the West "amounts to a revolution in consciousness, the crucial feature of which is the decision to distrust the evidence of our senses."[2] The resulting confusion is the mind/body split.

Classical historians often blame Plato and Aristotle for dividing the natural world from spiritual ideals, the Gnostics for separating heavenly and earthly realms, and early Christians for making war between the flesh and the spirit. Other researchers may castigate the French philosopher René Descartes (1596–1650) for disconnecting mental processes from the body.

However, these approaches tend to perpetuate the mind/body split. By formulating the problem as an intellectual mistake made in the past, we avoid taking responsibility for present-day behaviors that continue to leave us in pieces.

A growing number of researchers are convinced that the historical turns taken to split mind and body cannot be found solely in ancient arguments of philosophy and science. Rather, they believe we arrive at a better understanding by examining cultural habits such as food gathering, treatment of animals, gender roles, child rearing, grooming and the use of mirrors, and the visual representation of the human body (especially the female body) in religious and secular art.

To this list we need to add touch behavior. In our day, children receive little stimulation from family interaction and are more likely to develop a sense of mechanical touch from video machines programmed with war games. It is no wonder we see air force pilots returning from bombing missions and giving each other high fives on the runway. We have clergy molesting children, sex in the parish, and ritual and cultic abuse. In short, we are experiencing what psychologist Jules Older calls "touch gone wrong."[3] These behaviors present us not with a philosophical problem but with alarming signals of a widening gap between our right minds and our bodies.

In this chapter we will take a historical look at how we have waged this war on the body. By understanding how we have perpetuated a mind/body split, we will be better able to reconnect with a sense of the whole person.

During the first eight centuries after Christ, church members experienced *healing touch* in the sacraments and in their homes. In these settings they practiced the laying on of hands with oil blessed by the bishop. Then, gradually, through the Middle Ages both church and culture grew preoccupied with levels of authority (hierarchies), the very thing Jesus warned against (Matt. 20:25). In this period healing touch disappeared among the laity and became *power touch,* exercised by religious and political authorities. Later, with the birth of science in the sixteenth and seventeenth centuries, both healing touch and power touch were considered superstitions of the past, and *no touch* became the proper scientific philosophy. Finally, the unhealthy behavior modeled by no touch in helping professions, religious communities, and families produced *touch gone wrong.* Let's take a closer look at each of these periods.

Healing Touch

It is clear that Christians in the first eight centuries carried out in a variety of ways the healing ministry commissioned by Jesus. They expected healing not only in special services of the laying on of hands, exorcisms, and rituals involving relics of the saints, but also in baptisms, communions, and the use of oil for anointing in their homes.[4] According to church historian Charles W. Gusmer, the only liturgical texts on healing from this period

27

relate to the clergy's blessing of the oil that Christians took to their homes. Otherwise, rituals of healing touch using oil with the sick were performed by families as needed. "Just as the faithful would bring the eucharist home with them for communion during the week, so also would they take the blessed oil and apply it to themselves either through the form of drink ('taste') or through external application."[5] This was in no way a rite for the dying but witnessed to an incarnational way of living fully in the healing presence of Christ. Classical historian Peter Brown calls the early Christians' constant attention to healing an "obsessive compassion."[6]

Recipients of compassion were often those whom the Greek healing temples excluded, especially the dying. By the fourth century, Christians had established the first hospices and hospitals (*xenodochia*), sometimes in the remains of ancient temples.[7] Christians also attended to the poor. Professor Brown writes that "on Maundy Thursday, and on other feast days, the poor marched to the public baths, a new class of citizens, called to enjoy a new form of public benevolence. There they received a ritual wash and massage. As they went, they chanted the psalms of a high God, who was now thought to come closest . . . when the body was at its weakest."[8]

Integration of healing touch in the life of early Christian communities was probably nowhere more evident than in the training and reception of its new members. A thoroughgoing body awareness and rich tactile experience were built into this initiation.

After registering with the bishop, candidates for baptism spent one to three years in instruction as catechumenates. Afterward, for seven weeks before Easter, they fasted during the day, did not bathe, and abstained from sexual activity. During this time they attended worship as a group visible to the congregation. They had to be available for physical examination, for questions regarding their conduct, and for exorcism. As the candidates stood on rough sackcloth or animal skin, the exorcist named the evils they were turning away from as well as the kingdom they were about to enjoy more fully. Near the final days of this period, they memorized the creed summarizing their years of instruction.

Breaking the fast on Maundy Thursday, the catechumenates then had their feet washed by the bishop on Good Friday. On Easter Eve a vigil was kept in the dark of the sanctuary. With candles burning they recited the creed alone before the congregation. At dawn, forswearing the devil, candidates and congregation turned away from the night of the west to the light of the east. The baptistry was lit by candles and its curtain was withdrawn, exposing an octagonal pool with three steps leading down to waters often fed by a stream.

The catechumenates proceeded to the baptistry and were anointed from head to toe with oil. Their only clothing, a robe, was removed. Naked, they entered the water and were immersed three times according to the trinitarian formula. Afterward, still unclothed, these new Christians, now called "infantes," appeared before the bishop for confirmation. He gave them yet another anointing with oil, a laying on of hands, and a sign of the cross on the forehead. He clothed them in white linen and slippers and gave them milk and honey, "food for the newly born." In this new state they were allowed for the first time to receive the Holy Eucharist.

That Christians considered baptism a healing event demonstrates a wholesome use of touch and a profound notion of healing process. What was healing about baptism, in which touch played so significant a role? Certainly, abstaining from food and sex focused physical, emotional, and creative energies into new channels. Naming the evils from which to break free, a pivotal moment in any healing process, must have increased their choices of healthier lifestyles. A nurturing acceptance and blessing by new authority figures gave a network of support for new directions and expectations. Even vocational changes were expected.[9] Reflecting on this ritual, historical theologian Margaret R. Miles says that "the power of such a religious experience can only be imagined. . . . A change of beliefs and values . . . was not the only effect. A new integration of the body in religious commitment was produced."[10]

Power Touch

After A.D. 800, the clergy began to claim their official duties with a growing sense of self-importance. This development depended heavily on a hierarchical view of the world. At the top level were God, heaven, spirit, and men. On the bottom were the devil, hell, the body, and women. By the time of Thomas Aquinas (1225–1274) the shift to this hierarchical arrangement of power and authority was completed. In previous centuries when these levels were not so clearly delineated, the church could more easily embrace the mysteries of God's presence within the physical world—the message of incarnation. By Aquinas's time, God's relationship with the world and humanity's approach to divine realms occurred theoretically through an ordered chain of command.[11]

In this layered worldview, touch became a symbol of the interaction between levels. For example, bishops and popes installed kings with oil and the laying on of hands, conferring divine rights upon them. In a similar manner, clergy ordained candidates to the priesthood. Through touch, power was passed from higher levels to lower levels. This touch, which was more likely to be associated with administering levels of power than with facilitating the mysteries of God's presence within healing processes, is appropriately called *power touch.*

Power touch had a chilling effect on healing ministry. Healing touch, using oil in the homes, disappeared.[12] Soon the concept of healing would not refer to physical problems. The church maintained that, as far as healing was concerned, its interest was in the higher "spiritual cure," saving the soul. As early as the fifth century, Jerome (340–420) had changed the word "heal" in James 5:15 to mean "save."[13]

The consequences of this spiritualizing tendency were theologically and psychologically devastating. Theologians concluded that using healing touch on those with physical problems was something God meant only Jesus and his disciples to do. (Augustine held this view, though he changed his mind in his later years. However, most Christians, including the reformers,[14] accepted this notion, as do many today.) Left with no hands-on response to illness, theologians concluded that sickness must be God's way of dealing with sin. "Plague and indeed all epidemic diseases were . . . seen as the flood of God's wrath" in medieval times.[15] By the mid 1500s, physicians were required to discontinue treatment of patients who had not signed a confession after three days.[16]

Restricting healing to a purely spiritual arena created a disdain for the body. Because illness in the body was considered a sign of sin, the mere sight of medical realities of infirmity was thought to taint the clergy's soul.[17] Therefore, the feeling grew that it was more appropriate to put concerns for the body into the hands of physicians, whose guilds were emerging at this time. Physical complaints were also brought to kings, whose "royal touch" was thought to cure diseases, a custom popular in France and England between the tenth and eighteenth centuries.[18] In avoiding symptoms of the sick, the clergy by and large kept themselves from direct patient contact, except at the time of death.

In the years between 800 and 1300 we see the disappearance of liturgies and rituals aimed at healing the whole person. At best, "unction for healing became unction for dying."[19] Oil and the laying on of hands were used in the rite of extreme unction to administer forgiveness of sin and usher the person to a higher spiritual abode, thus exemplifying power touch. Such a use of touch was not to be interpreted as a means of bringing together body, mind, and spirit on the occasion of a serious but nonterminal episode.

What then happened confirms our suspicion that the deep human capacity for expressing compassion through healing touch cannot be taken away without repercussions. Indeed, something much more profound and hidden was occurring. The repression of healing and compassion fueled the reach of power touch to the extreme. How else can we explain the papal legalization of torture (1252) to carry out the grisly business of the Inquisition (instituted in 1233)? How much compassion had to be squelched in order to grasp hold of the weapons for the

bloody Crusades (1100–1300)? How many persons on the social fringes between 1200 and 1500 could have been blessed
instead of burned? Hands used not for healing but for cranking
the racks, butchering the infidels, and burning the witches
shaped *"the origins of the modern police state,"* according to
historian Morris Berman.[20]

In these events we can easily see that the next logical step
after power touch would be touch gone wrong. However, this
progression was interrupted by a curious but revealing moment
in the history of touch—the philosophy of no touch.

No Touch

The road from power touch to touch gone wrong proceeded
through the rise of science and its no-touch philosophy. By the
end of the Reformation, power touch was no longer seen as a
valid symbol of authority. In the Roman Catholic Church, healing liturgies had ceased by the middle of the 1500s, not to be
considered again until the 1960s. Royal touch by kings was on
the wane and would disappear by the end of the 1700s.

The hierarchies that so neatly ordered heaven and earth
and that were mediated through power touch were being dis-
mantled. As power was dispersed to the people through literacy
and better access to market economies, what counted was not
divine right but numbers of dollars and votes. In religion what
mattered was not spiritual mysteries but the written and
preached word. In science the goal was no longer to achieve
an alchemical union of spirit and matter but to separate matter
into units whose workings could be predicted and controlled.[21]
A universe ordered by the power of the mind is a universe that
does not need touch.

A watershed figure in the rise of this thoroughgoing rational-
istic approach was Marin Mersenne (1588–1648), a Franciscan
priest in Paris. Mersenne's *Harmonie universelle* (1636) in-
spired an international community of intellectuals with the
wonder of mathematics. Mersenne believed precise measure-

ment could explain everything from the grace of God to the king's ability to cure by "the royal touch."[22] According to Mersenne, the true physician would have to be fundamentally a musician, since he would be able mathematically to correlate the soul's sickness with the harmonies of the heavens.[23] Note how Mersenne's ideal physician is ultimately oriented to what cannot be touched (the soul) and theoretically has no need to touch, except to gather data.

In the scientific era, measuring substituted for touching. With accurate data on the body, one could predict even moral behavior, according to the father of statistics and inventor of the concept of the "average man," Adolphe Quetelet (1796–1874).[24]

By the time of Freud, it must have seemed that Mersenne's ideal of measuring even the soul of a person could be achieved without touch. In the early part of Freud's career, he would touch the patient's forehead or hand and then release the touch to encourage recall of memories. Freud soon abandoned the use of this "pressure technique" because of "the desire of the early analysts to establish themselves as scientists."[25] A very few psychotherapists continued to use touch through the lineage of Wilhelm Reich and Alexander Lowen, but no-touch technique remained the standard among the vast majority of therapists.[26]

The standard continues into modern time. In the medical community, the research of psychologist Jules Older speaks for itself. Out of the 169 English-speaking medical schools he surveyed in the 1980s, only 12 gave any formal training in touch.[27] In mainline religion, we have never integrated this subject intentionally in any form of Christian education, as far as I know. Somehow a pastoral counseling profession was built on a base of clinical training that did not deal intentionally with touch.[28] We have even produced professional journals on pastoral care[29] and liturgical resources for healing services[30] that never discuss the importance of touch.

Power touch and no touch grew out of men's domination of the economic and religious market for health care—a goal achieved at women's expense. While men were entitled to education and access to physicians' guilds, women and peasants were more than likely to be considered nonconformists, heretics, and werewolves doing the work of the devil. When one third of Europe's population was decimated by the plague of the Black Death in the middle 1300s, who but women, thought to have caused the fall and its consequence of death, would be blamed? In *Witches, Midwives, and Nurses: A History of Women Healers,* historians Barbara Ehrenreich and Deidre English write that the reach for power in the late Middle Ages resulted in a "ruling class campaign of terror directed against the female peasant population."[31] This reign of terror was in particular a check on women healers. "In an era of male domination in all matters of life except healing, men in power began systematically persecuting women and designating them witches to maintain a male monopoly over the profitable enterprise of healing."[32]

From this deeper philosophical perspective, no touch and power touch are essentially the same thing. Only the roles have changed. In the era of no touch, instead of clergy and kings representing the cultural ideal, we have scientists and counselors. True, modern-day advocates of no touch are hardly as brazen as their witch-hunting predecessors. Nonetheless, as long as males monopolize the medium, the message tends to denigrate women.[33]

The denigration was hardly subtle in the case of James B. Watson, father of American behaviorism. In his popular book *Psychological Care of Infant and Child* (1928), he advised mothers not to touch their children: "It may tear the heart strings a bit, this thought of stopping the tender outward demonstration of your love for your children or of their love for you. But if you are convinced that this is best for the child, aren't you willing to stifle a few pangs?" And what if a woman is not willing? She is, said Watson, "starved for love. [Touching would be] a sex-seeking response in her."[34]

The message conveyed in power touch and no touch alike is ultimately oppressive. Basically, Watson's doctrine continues the medieval view that set males on thrones in the heavens and chained females to the evils of the earth.[35] Not peculiar to Christianity, this idea nonetheless was evident even in the church's happiest holistic moments. To prepare for baptism in the early centuries, women were placed last in line and required to wear their hair down, symbolizing respectively their place on the lowest rung of the created order and their responsibility for sin.[36] In this context, whatever else religious touch conveyed, it also reinforced male control.

There is a direct parallel in the ways both touch and visual practices in Christian tradition were made to serve the agenda of male power. After careful analysis of both the production and content of Christian art until the fourteenth century, Professor Miles finds that "not a single image of any woman . . . was designed or created by a woman. The images we must deal with represent a male response to a woman, a male way of relating to women, and a male way of communicating with women."[37] The consequences of this kind of visual practice are the spiritualizing of women as a way of distancing and managing them; the increasing fear of women; the projection onto women of the causes of the fall, evil, sin, and death; the scapegoating of women for physical and social problems such as plagues; and the blaming of women for lust arising in men.[38]

These results are strikingly similar to what happens when touch is divorced from healing and linked solely with power (in whatever form), implying subordination of the receiver: controlling touch to maintain domination, lack of touch based on fear of intimacy and possibly compensated for by heightened verbal or other means of control, abusive touch based on anger stemming from shame or anxiety about one's self-esteem, or harassing touch that sexualizes relationships and accuses the other for provoking such behavior.

What happens to healing touch under the masculine oppression of power touch and no touch? Briefly, it was women's historical resistance to these attempted usurpations of touch and to philosophies ranking them low in the created order that kept healing touch alive.

In U.S. history, women's protests created healing systems

outside the control of established medicine and religion. Using direct access to divine energies as prescribed in natural—or "harmonial"—philosophies, they could easily make end runs around orthodox churches and science.

Unorthodox religious groups native to America—Christian Scientists,[39] Seventh-Day Adventists, Mormons, Jehovah's Witnesses, and Pentecostals—"have all had strong interest in religious healing"[40] and often featured some form of feminine healing touch. The first two organized around the healing experiences and visions of women: Mary Baker Eddy (1821–1910) and Ellen Gould White (1827–1911). Women healers such as Maria B. Woodworth-Etter and Aimee Semple McPherson were also prominent in the emergence of various strands of Pentecostals at the turn of the century. Woodworth-Etter's healing touch induced in some worshipers a trancelike state called "slain in the Spirit" or "resting in Jesus."

Women figured significantly in efforts to reclaim healing ministry within mainline denominations in this century. Ethel Tulloch played a prominent role in the beginnings of the International Order of St. Luke the Physician in the early 1900s. Loosely connected to this order as an intensive training resource is the School of Pastoral Care begun by Agnes Sanford. The Methodists' New Life Clinic became well known through the ministry of Olga Worrell. She allowed researchers to study the effects of her healing touch.

The healing experience of Mary Caroline ("Myrtle") Fillmore (1845–1931) resulted in the founding of the Unity Church in 1889.[41] Spiritualists communing with the departed were mainly women.[42] They practiced passes of the hand over the body to effect an unobstructed flow of "spirit" or "vital fluid" in the body. They are the direct forerunners of modern "parapsychology . . . psychical research . . . New Age trance channeling, Eckankar, the Association for Research and Enlightenment, crystal healing, and attempts to link Eastern meditational practices with contemporary American concerns."[43]

Commenting on the rise of these movements in the United States, Morton Kelsey theorizes that "had the mainline churches been more open theologically, the healing movement might have been integrated in them. But in view of [the churches'] hostility toward the subject, the movement had to go forward on its own."[44]

It is due to this largely feminine stream resisting the monopoly of "masculine facts" that we see today a resurgence of interest in healing touch. We are now hearing "from the limbs that got hacked off,"[45] as Morris Berman puts it. In the decade of the 1980s perhaps the clearest sign for renewed interest in healing touch was the exponential rise in the supply and demand for professional bodyworkers such as massage therapists.[46] That a growing number of these professionals are clergy indicates that the movement presents an opportunity to take seriously religion's relationship to the healing arts. In addition, some pastoral educators are now saying that they *should* be offering instruction in touch.[47] Mainline denominations are now making available liturgical supplements for services of pastoral care with "laying on of hands." Several theologians, such as Jürgen Moltmann and James B. Nelson, have begun to address the mind/body split. They remind us of the dialogue between body and soul and thus keep before us the balanced perspective we have missed in the past.

These positive developments come none too soon for the consequences of power-touch and no-touch philosophies are upon us. When our own Senate Judicial Committee declares that the United States is "the most violent and self-destructive nation on earth,"[48] one cannot help but wonder: Did the historical phase in which we experimented with no touch in medicine, families, and congregations contribute to the problem? Whatever we conclude, we cannot look back on no touch as a particularly enlightened moment of our past. Rather, as part of a "society addicted to control,"[49] it points to an abuse of power. The abuse often happens through touch.

Touch Gone Wrong

It is no secret that ours is a violent society. The United States leads the industrial world in executions, slaughter of animals, interventionary wars, homicide rates, and mass murders.[50] Add to this record the daily supply of violent images through the media (an estimated 100,000 from TV viewed by age eighteen), and we begin to understand the extent to which abusive touch fits our way of life. Millions of Americans preach and practice applying the rod in the name of God and see no reason to stop there. As a result, a surprisingly large percentage of the population, especially women and children, suffers from physical, sexual, or ritual or cultic abuse.

In a violent male-dominated society, touch is most likely to go wrong when men are provided position and power by virtue of their gender, their access to women's and children's bedrooms and psyches, and the privacy that protects men's domestic and professional activities. Family settings and professional ministry are the arenas that consistently meet these conditions.

Regarding family settings, the American experience of discipline in the home is graphically described by Philip Greven in *Spare the Child.*[51] He reports how parents, especially fathers, used hands, rods, belts, and other instruments on children. Their purpose was, and still is, to break the child's will. Their rationale is that such discipline saves children from eternal punishment. Corporal punishment was a common and in some cases daily experience for the children of Jonathan Edwards ("the most articulate . . . defender of eternal punishment in American history"). Others, such as Aimee Semple McPherson, Billy Graham, Oral Roberts, and Kathryn Kuhlman, also experienced this sort of treatment in childhood.[52] Though preaching the rod is more audible among the Fundamentalists, the use of it is found almost everywhere.

Greven sees in this historical tradition "a subtle but constant escalation of levels of coercion, force, assault, violence, pain, and suffering."[53] As church and society, we have yet to understand the connection between the hickory stick and our wrathful theologies, militant authoritarianism, and increasing reliance on violent solutions to private and public problems. But there is no doubt in Greven's mind that "physical punishment [is] the archetype of many other forms of assault and battery."[54]

Others count the cost of this "poisonous pedagogy."[55] Pamela Cooper-White, who works with battered women, reports that "one out of three women in the U.S. is raped; one out of four . . . is battered by an intimate partner; at least one out of four has been abused as a child; and at least one out of five is an incest survivor."[56]

Likewise, in professional ministry the conditions are hazardous for those who touch, especially for men. In the research for their book *Sex in the Parish,* Karen Lebacqz and Ronald Barton found that most clergy relied on their feelings, instincts, and intuitions to help them keep proper boundaries with parishioners. However, the authors emphasize that factors built into professional ministry—behavior of mentors, strength of one's primary relationship, easy access to other relationships, and privacy—were probably more determinative of behavior than good intentions.[57] This is so, they reason, because instincts and intentions themselves can be culturally conditioned by such factors. Living in a warped society means "the intuitions that it fosters will also be warped."[58] Thus it is likely that women clergy will find reliable guidance within themselves more than men, whose feeling levels are more vulnerable to the culture's conditioning.

We need to recognize that while both men and women are naturally capable of providing healing touch, the cultural conditions that predispose to abusive touch overwhelmingly apply to men. As experience with power touch and no touch shows, men have associated touch for a long time with positions of power and authority, with the need to control both people and processes, and with sexual agenda. This psychic inheritance can lead men in modern helping professions to find touch a convenient link between fantasy and "sex in the forbidden zone" (title of a book by psychiatrist Peter Rutter). Rutter estimates that "96 percent . . . of sexual exploitation by professionals occurs between a man in power and a woman under his care."[59] Though no firm statistics exist for determining the incidence of sexual contact between clergy and parishioners, Marie Fortune states that "there is no reason to assume [the incidence] is any less frequent than the 10–15% for other counseling professions."[60] Furthermore, since research shows that counselors "who became sexual with patients also engaged in more 'non-erotic' physical contact with patients,"[61] encouraging any kind of touch without awareness of these cultural conditionings is not only naive but dangerous.

The problem that affects both sexes but especially men in such a culture is, according to Rutter, difficulty in feeling compassion. Preoccupied with his own wounds, a man is "continually asking the woman to minister to him."[62] Without a doubt this message can be communicated by men or women nonverbally, through touch. To be liberated from such compulsivity requires new values operating in social arrangements and inner life. Not until men and women value mutuality more than control in relation to the opposite sex (as well as in relation to opposite sexual aspects of their own personalities) will they be able to get past wounded hearts to compassionate ones. When that happens, touch is ready to link the compassionate heart of the wounded healer to healing processes.

Advocating healing touch does not mean simply calling for more touch without regard for the possibility that such behavior may add to existing destructive patterns. Nor do we support reaction to the opposite extreme in such anxious caution that we merely perpetuate our fears. We need "not less but a different kind of touch,"[63] says Julie Dennison, body therapist and mission director in the Evangelical Lutheran Church in America. She is talking about the kind of touch that moves beyond the touch gone wrong which historically has attended male privilege.

In terms of our history of touch behavior, what we see in touch gone wrong is the cumulative effect of the oppression of power touch and the propaganda of no touch. Everyone suffers. Call women's bodies into question, and children's bodies are no good either; allegedly, beating is the only thing that will save them. In addition, keep women from touching, and children grow into shamed and angry adults with little memory of healing touch and plenty of touch gone wrong stored in their bodies.

Resentful and split from the goodness of our bodies, we cannot hear the body's language of compassion. Instead, the body becomes our enemy. Only its loudest signal, the sexual one, may get through. If so, we are quick to equate body and sex. Touch can then only be understood as sexually controlling.

However, sex is not the basic issue in touch gone wrong. The core of abuse is "an imbalance of power . . . and [the] need to reinforce and heighten the intensity of that power dynamic."[64] Maintaining this unbalanced power dynamic depends on perpetuating women's self-understanding "as a nurturing, sexual servant class."[65] In such a society the first issue about touching is not "whether it is good or bad," says Anne Wilson Schaef. "The issue is whether touching or non-touching are [sic] used for control and whether control is seen as good and necessary." As long as this remains unclear, therapies utilizing touch "are not healing people. Instead, they are fostering co-dependence and preparing people to fit into an addictive society."[66] When touch serves this purpose, it has gone wrong indeed.

Conclusion

The mind/body split occurs whenever the body—or any of its systems, such as vision or touch—is controlled by power's agenda. Power itself is not the villain. Rather, the problem lies in an exclusive pairing of touch with power. Whenever touch is tied solely to its results, the ego's self-understanding is more likely to be tied—some say addicted—to its image of control. *To have the world at one's fingertips is the agenda of power.*

In this regard, alternative medicine and religion, as well as New Age bodywork and touch therapies, are no different from their established competitors. These nontraditional practitioners merely seek to get us to wholeness or heaven more directly, more cheaply, and with fewer side effects. But the emphasis is the same—a fascination with, and addiction to, greater degrees of efficacy, power, and control.

The biblical metaphor for this fascination with absolute

manual control is "overreaching," "grabbing for more and more"—literal meanings of the word *pleonexia*. Its core concept is "ruthless, aggressive self-assertion." It is translated in the New Testament as "greed" (Luke 12:15) and "covetousness" (Rom. 1:29). It is equated with "idolatry" (Eph. 5:5; Col. 3:5) and "extortion" (2 Cor. 9:5). Referring to the hand, *pleonexia* expresses perfectly how touch or holding, a natural and powerful function, might be used by the self in an insatiable grasp for more.

Healing touch does not seek to control. It cares about both its intentions and the consequences of its actions but does not tie its ego to results. It prays for curing but is not finished when curing is accomplished or impossible. It seeks to be obedient and a channel of compassion and thus to facilitate a healing process larger than its capacity to control.

In the absence of the model of healing touch, the techniques of power touch and no touch—which often, indeed, serve useful purposes—may easily become touch gone wrong. Reclaiming healing touch means basically that we come to grips, so to speak, with addictions to power. It means we loosen our grip and reach out from compassion, not compulsion.

At the heart of faith communities with such a somatic integrity is a respect for the slow, alchemical fires of the healing process. The work Jesus commissioned us to carry out, and which our bodies naturally enjoy, calls for touching that facilitates the healing process. This dynamic is not under our control but awaits our joyful, obedient participation—and our understanding.

CHAPTER 3

The Language
of Healing Touch

Healing touch is possible only after we have loosened our grip, after we have let go of grasping. As theologian Walter Brueggemann puts it, "When we get free of coveting [*pleonexia*], the power to interact in healing ways surprises us."[1]

Letting go, however, does not mean flipping to the other extreme and giving up all sense of responsibility. The tendency to fluctuate between opposing behaviors in this manner is noticeable even in the way we use our hands. According to Gerald G. May, psychiatrist and spiritual director, "When we become overly self-conscious and pre-occupied, our hands turn into jerky, contrived things that grasp and claw, clench and shove, meddle and manipulate. . . . At still other times we sit on our hands, forcibly and brutally preventing their movement." The issue is excessive willfulness in relation to power, the first extreme "exaggerating and aggrandizing personal power, and the latter . . . forcibly denying and restricting it."[2]

A more balanced ministry is about the sharing and coordinating of divine/human energies and powers. As Clyde W. Ford so effectively describes in his book *Where Healing Waters Meet*, touch brings two people together in a healing journey as guide and traveler. This mutuality is not conveyed by the usual terms, "doctor/patient, practitioner/client, therapist/client, healer/healee . . . in which . . . only one party has the power."[3]

In healing touch we listen accurately to share the traveler's pain. In response, we *coordinate our hearts with our hands* to share compassion through touch. Since Jesus modeled this way for us, we trust that what we do is part of a larger *healing process* guided by God. When, as a result, we become more balanced personally and communally, we see evidence that the process leads to greater *health and wholeness.*

The three areas just emphasized give us language crucial to Christian healing ministry. As we discuss each one, let's keep in mind the image of open hands sharing power rather than clenched fists tightening the controls.

Health and Wholeness

Of all the biblical words related to health and wholeness, the one around which most of the others cluster is shalom. In the Old Testament, this term depends on the exodus as the defining event that reveals God's character to save and heal Israel and thus give it shalom (see Lev. 26:3–6). The vision of shalom is not a sectarian one. It extends beyond Israel so that "all of creation is one, every creature in community with every other, living in harmony and security toward the joy and well-being of every other creature."[4] Such a comprehensive expectation means that shalom and salvation share similar meanings (Isa. 52:7). But the kernel of shalom is communal harmony.

Health is only one characteristic of shalom, which also includes security, prosperity, and a long and happy life. So whenever we talk about the Hebrew roots of health we must picture the individual in community, which in turn is being saved by God for the realization of shalom. While health is subsumed under the larger meanings of shalom and salvation in the Old Testament generally, the link between health and salvation does become more noticeable in the later prophets (see Isa. 53:5 and Jer. 8:22).

The convergence of health and salvation begun by the prophets becomes explicit in the New Testament (Luke 4:18). In the Gospels the incarnation of God in Christ brought shalom: "Peace I leave with you" (John 14:27). Physical healing becomes the centerpiece for the demonstration of shalom. The title for Jesus, *soter,* means both savior and healer. Consistent with his Hebrew roots, Jesus linked healing with shalom (Mark

5:34) and thus with restoration to community, especially for those whose impairments had severed their communal connections (Mark 2:17).

We see shalom manifested in Jesus' life in many ways, not the least of which is his touch. Through touch Jesus builds community and embodies a healthy sharing of power. We have already referred to many stories in which Jesus releases power for healing (Luke 4:40). In these healings his receptivity to faith contributed by the sick person (Matt. 9:29) and by friends of the sick (Matt. 9:2) is very evident. In addition, Jesus welcomes children to be touched (Mark 9:35–37; 10:13–16), the woman sinner and her expensive ointment (Luke 7:36–50), the disciple Thomas's need to touch in order to believe (John 20:26–29), and even Judas's kiss (Mark 14:45). The sharing of power was especially conspicuous in Jesus' choosing to touch the powerless and the untouchables—the demon-possessed (Luke 8:26–33), the lepers (Mark 1:40–45), the lame, blind, poor, and others disrespected by society. We see in Jesus' touch behavior, which demonstrates a nonpatronizing compassion for the physical as well as the social dimensions of illness, the kind of health and wholeness envisioned in shalom.

To the kernel of community in shalom, Jesus' ministry adds a here-and-now urgency. Shalom is not only a vision of the unity of all things but unfolds now in our midst in specific instances of healing. For this reason the combined Old and New Testament notion of health contains a double meaning. It is a symbol of the unity (wholeness) of all things in God's saving purposes, and it also refers to the historical realities of healing (health). The expression "health and wholeness" reflects this twofold nature.

On the basis of the biblical notion of shalom, revealed so clearly in the touch behavior of Jesus, we may define health and wholeness as *cooperation with the Creator for reorganizing unbalanced aspects of life in order to live more deeply integrated personally and communally.* In this definition, "cooperation" is exercised by both individuals and communities. "Unbalanced" refers to physical impairments, behavioral dysfunctions, social injustices, and ecological problems. Lives that are integrated "personally" involve physical, mental and emotional, and spiritual aspects of the whole person. Similarly, to be more integrated "communally" means we are always engaged on ecological, economic, and ecumenical levels.

This biblical definition is more holistic than popular Western understandings of health and wholeness. Generally, these theories focus on overcoming physical or social impairment (function), coping with stress that originates internally or externally (adaptation), and integrating deeper aspects of the self (development).[5]

Restoring or improving function is the chief concern of Western medicine and the helping professions. While this goal encompasses a myriad of practical ways to prevent and cure diseases and relieve organic and emotional bases of distress, it often lacks an articulated norm or vision of what is proper functioning. Thus, it is apt to impose norms purely in terms of functionality, such as extending life for a few weeks with an artificial heart or by some other technical means. Such "solutions" may in fact cause more suffering.

The theories of health that encourage adaptation to our environment build on the principle of homeostasis—the organism's ability to compensate and balance its internal and external states. Adaptation theories often preach a peace-of-mind philosophy that overlooks radical evil or calls it illusory. Thus it devalues the capacity for risking one's "steady state" to aim for greater integration. Also overlooked is the important role that suffering might play in such growth.

Developmentalists nurture processes of growth, recovery, transformation, and rehabilitation. They contribute greatly to our understanding of healing process. However, any theory that relies so heavily on a person's seemingly unlimited capacity for personal growth eventually runs headlong into the stark realities of tragedy and suffering (such as addiction) which severely limit human choice. In such cases healing may require some form of intervention that an individual may have little or no capacity to initiate.

While each of these theories makes a contribution to our understanding of health, each also has limited application. They almost always are oriented toward the health of the individual and tend to overlook the possibility that "a society may also be ill."[6] We need to be guided by an understanding of health and wholeness that reconnects people not only to their bodies and psyches but to meaningful relationship to God, to one another, and to the earth.

Healing Process

Guided by a biblical notion of health and wholeness, we see that healing process applies to moments in life that threaten our communal destiny for shalom. For many people the opportunity for healing begins with physical infirmity or impairment. For others life may feel interrupted by some twist of unexpected good fortune or simply by the onset of natural biological and social stages. Regardless of the occasion, a common thread in these experiences is loss of familiar structures (even dysfunctional ones) that define one's world—loss of one's shalom.

The beginning of healing for Moses and the Israelites was their struggle against slavery; for Paul it was a blinding light; for Gopi Krishna the shattering experience of kundalini. For some it might be a divorce or the death of a loved one. For me it was losing a job at thirty-five years of age.

Primal rage mixed with shame filled every corner of my being. I felt I would never fulfill my calling. As a househusband for the next year, I busied myself with various things around the kitchen. To my surprise I enjoyed some of these tasks, especially making bread. I realized I was developing the feminine side of my psyche. Finally, when I became a hospital chaplain, I was able to put my greater awareness of loss and the skills of nurturing to practical use. I was encouraged to believe that "all things work together for good" (Rom. 8:28).

Reading over the journal I kept during this time, I began to sense a threefold structure in my experience of healing. It consisted of a chaotic time of feeling rejected and alone, a period of personal discoveries and insights, and then the joyful opportunities to integrate these learnings into a more compassionate life. The threefoldness rang a familiar biblical bell in my mind: faith, hope, and love. I am now convinced that these words, their sequence and associated behaviors, contain the secrets of the healing process.[7]

Amen is one form of the Hebrew root aman, "believe," which originally meant to be carried or firmly held by a nurse or a caregiver.[8] Nothing better describes this first part of healing process. One feels as helpless as a child, totally powerless, and needing to be carried, comforted, and consoled. One also feels as emotionally volatile as a child crying out in distress and anger, questioning the justice and fairness of life. From the point of view of someone "faithing it" the experience feels as though shalom is all but forgotten.

Surprises occur in the second phase. Hope is like that—unexpectedly cropping up in the midst of despair. Resentment mysteriously subsides. New interests emerge. Friends rearrange themselves, some sticking closer, some leaving. Trust can be attempted, but not yet in total confidence. This middle period is rather dangerous, like a roller coaster. Abruptly one may feel yanked back to square one. Maybe that is why faith and hope are often used in combination in the Bible. There is a back-and-forth dynamic between them, like the giant pistons turning the wheels of an old locomotive. In relation to the wheels, the pistons of faith and hope seem to be merely going back and forth, while in reality they are driving the engine forward, to new space and time. So hope is akin to waiting, believing that the pain is not for nothing and leads to smoother terrain.

The vision of shalom is the fuel for this engine. We never really lose it, residing as it does in every cell of our bodies. Hope is the flame that enables the memories and realities of shalom to be perceived in new, unexpected ways. Forged in the fires of faith and hope, the new perspective, the renewed ego, the changed behaviors, and the energized community slowly prove their trustworthiness. One can step out again, less defensive, more discerning, compassionate, and loving.

In the third phase, the love now given is deeper and wiser. One often joins with those who suffer in ways similar to one's own story, as in Alcoholics Anonymous, hospice programs, and a variety of volunteer and support groups. In this process of giving and receiving it is not easy to tell who is really the healer and who is the healee. When love flows, it refreshes all and reminds us that both giver and receiver are ultimately sustained by the same grace (See Appendix A, Reflection Sheet No. 1: Healing Process).

To test the validity of this perception of healing process, compare it with the archetypal saving and healing events in the Bible. It begins with a group who felt very cut off from membership in the human community, the Hebrew slaves. The forerunners—Abraham, Isaac, Jacob—set examples of faith by stepping out in directions totally separate from their kindred, and separated they became, eventually, as laborers under Pharaoh. Moses, whose life was rudely interrupted by Yahweh, became the reluctant liberator. Yet he was not as reluctant as his followers. During the break from Egypt, their complaints were fairly characteristic of faith behavior. The known realities of servitude often seemed preferable to the unknowns of the wilderness.

Nevertheless, in this forty-year middle phase they discovered much that gave them hope. They found a name for themselves. They learned the Ten Commandments.

Finally, they entered the promised land. There they practiced loving God and neighbor as self, always remembering that they were once strangers themselves. Later, of course, the whole process would be played out again in the exile, learning to sing a new song and returning with a new covenant of the heart.

In Jesus' experience the definitive test of faith was the crucifixion. In the next scenario (which never received much canonical press: 1 Peter 3:19; 4:6) hope emerged, curiously enough, in the descent into hell. Nonetheless, this phase conforms to the pattern of reintegrating the lost or forgotten parts—in this case a reunion with the dead who had gone before him. Finally, in the resurrection Jesus returned to bring the prize of shalom based on the victory of love over the forces of evil and death.

As we shall see in chapter 6, the same tripartite structure in the Gospel accounts helps us interpret the beginning of Jesus' mission—baptism, wilderness, ministry. In turn, these texts offer insight into the shape of early Christian worship—baptism, confirmation, communion. No doubt this communal experience shaped the discussion of Christian life in terms of faith, hope, and love by Paul (Rom. 5:1–5), by Evagrius Ponticus (A.D. 346–399), and by Augustine (A.D. 354–430). As these stages often involved physical trials, new ways of thinking, and new attitudes, they became associated respectively with body, mind, and spirit. Thus, in Eastern Christianity spiritual practice became known as the prayers of the lips, mind, and heart; in the West, the purgative, illuminative, and unitive disciplines.[9]

Christians did not invent threefold healing and transformational process. Joseph Campbell found this pattern common to classic hero myths. "The hero follows the pattern: a separation from the world, a penetration to some source of power, and a life-enhancing return."[10] Jungian analyst Edward Edinger writes that such a threefold pattern is repeated many times throughout one's lifetime. The ego is wrenched loose from its familiar identifications and undergoes a traumatic period ("conflict," "fall"), often associated with guilt. There follows a time of alienation and suffering ("wilderness," "sacrifice"), through which one comes in touch with deeper potentials of the Self or Divine. Finally, the person moves into a more integrated awareness of the whole person. The goal of the process is "to redeem . . . the hidden Self."[11]

Fortunately, these common patterns in healing process are well known in the counseling profession. In *The Skilled Helper,* Gerard Egan integrates anthropological research both with the work of Carl Rogers and with R. R. Carkuff's three-stage model to offer valuable commentary on healing process for helping professionals.[12] William Bridges's *Transitions: Making Sense of Life's Changes* builds on the work of Arnold van Gennep in *Rites of Passage* and is one of the most helpful books to put in the hands of clients or anyone struggling with life's radical dislocations.[13] The most thorough discussion of the dynamics of threefold healing process in terms of pastoral theology is the classic text by James N. Lapsley, *Salvation and Health.*[14] When changes occur, faith struggles initially with issues of identity and self-worth. The mode of defense against change is what Lapsley calls "maintenance." Only by lowering this defense can one let go and risk taking up the next task of development. Reducing the tension between maintenance and development is at least part of the meaning and effect of forgiveness (including self-acceptance). The whole process leads to a third level of greater health called "participation." Offering excellent insight into the nature of healing process, Lapsley's model is designed to be more comprehensive than a mere discussion of three phases.

A review of the literature on threefold healing process yields at least six abiding principles worth noting.

First, *each phase has its own integrity and takes its own time.* Faith's honest struggling, though not easy, cannot be hurried. The whys need to be articulated and dealt with, as Pierre Wolff does so sensitively in his gem of a little book, *May I Hate God?*[15] The tension between holding on ("maintenance") and letting go ("development") as described by Lapsley takes time before one senses movement to new ground. The passion of the earlier stages of faith and hope must find some resolution before the compassion of the later stages of hope and love can emerge. Respecting the integrity of each phase prevents undo anxiety caused by trying to hurry up the process or by taking on additional responsibilities (for the sake of "love"), when what he or she needs to do is to receive (in faith) or wait for a while (in hope).

Second, *the healing process as a whole has its own integrity.* The integrity of each phase, as just discussed, does not imply that each is separate. In fact, no stage is ever finally left behind. Rather, like a telescope, one segment slides within the next, lending its viewpoint to enlarge one's perspective. The total process moves from a receiving mode (faith) into deeper intra- and interpersonal realms of reconciliation and sharing (hope) to a more giving and caring attitude (love). This truth should not be misused to deny painful realities. ("Cheer up, you're just going through a phase.") But when properly understood and communicated (often through touch), it can counter the sense of suffering as never-ending. Knowledge that the painful feelings of faith and the sometimes stressful waits in hope are as important as the selfless givings of love strengthens the whole person throughout the healing process. As a result, we bring both our wounds and our wisdom to see more clearly the next steps we need to take. Healers who are formed by this process will always be wounded healers.

Third, *healing in one dimension can bring about healing in another.* A woman whose cat dies experiences a loss. Her sorrow triggers a childhood memory of the death of her father, for whom she never finished grieving. Reaching into her Christian heritage for support, she identifies with Jesus at the point where he felt forsaken by his Father. She realizes how long it has been since she felt close to God and finds renewed interest in discussing her spiritual journey in a church sharing group. Thus the healing process is never an absolutely private affair. It always has implications for the larger self and the greater community of which one is a part.

Fourth, *healing processes are never-ending.* While healing process around a particular event may yield at some point a sense of closure and become a chapter (and thus a great resource) in a person's or a community's life, we may assume that some form of healing process is always occurring on some level.

Fifth, *healing process works through (not around) the resistance of opposing processes.* A threefold process underlies Gerald G. May's discussion of the classic resistance of addiction.[16] In May's favorite metaphor of the hand, addiction begins by tensing one's grip (on substances, relationships, images of self or God). Driven by fear during this learning phase, the fist provides security in specific circumstances. To extend this behavior in order to find relief in a variety of stressful situations, one merely tightens one's grip (on whatever is addicting). But by doing so one has also tightened one's bondage in relation to these addictive objects. This is the second phase of habit formation. Finally, such behavior develops its own autonomy and becomes inappropriate, precipitating crises in the real world—the third phase of struggle. The sets of opposites in relation to healing process are noteworthy: faith/fear, hope/bondage, love/crises. May's discussion of how a threefold healing process counters the resistance of such opposing forces is the best I know for discerning the course healing takes through *pleonexia* to a more integrated sense of the whole person.

Sixth, *knowledge of healing process in ourselves increases the likelihood of being effective facilitators of healing in others.* Familiarity with the healing process helps us own the seasons of our lives, as Ecclesiastes teaches, and to anticipate the shape of future healing moments—for example, around retirement. The point here is not to predict and control the process but to anticipate best how to cooperate with God, who directs it, in order to facilitate healing in ourselves and others. Sensitivity to where one is on his or her healing journey and where others are who receive our care is crucial in discerning whether to touch and, if so, how. We will discuss these discernment and referral skills more thoroughly in chapters 4 and 5.

The best way to explore the dynamics of healing process is to find these moments in your own life. Go back to a time when you experienced a significant loss. List all the feelings you remember being churned up at the onset. Who and what comforted you most in those days? Next, reflect on the period during which you began to feel some movement through the trials. How did you begin making sense of it all? Describe the times you found some healing from the loss—persons you forgave, anger you resolved, and so on. Finally, look at what you learned from the whole experience. Count your blessings: the gains that came from the pain, the lessons that continue to shape your life and make you wiser, more compassionate.

A special benefit of recalling past journeys through loss or illness into greater wholeness is the awareness it brings of the many resources that support healing process. For example, in the struggles of faith we use the prayers of confession, lamentation, and petition. Waiting for hope we may practice meditation or conversational prayer. Also, for putting the pieces together during this "in-between" time, prayer methods using creative visualization and focusing are fruitful.[17] Prayers of thanksgiving are the hallmark of hope, celebrating the gifts and gains that help us make it through the dark nights. Finally, in love we give voice to our compassion through intercession for others. Contemplation and silence are also prayer forms; they bring balance and perspective to the work of love.

In addition to prayer, many other resources in Christian heritage support healing. Excellent books on this subject have been written by Kenneth L. Bakken and Kathleen H. Hofeller, Bill Ratliff, and John A. Sanford,[18] and you may identify many other resources from your own experience. Just brainstorm the kinds of activities, art, colors, food, movements, music, people, or postures that you associate with faith, hope, or love. Then arrange them appropriately along the healing process in a manner similar to the prayer forms just mentioned.

The same method is also useful for examining how touch facilitates healing. First, brainstorm as many different kinds of touch as you can remember in your life. Then, using the framework of healing process, identify which forms of touch you would associate with specific phases of healing. For example, we associate an arm around a shoulder with encouraging someone's faith in times of grief, a high five with celebrating a hopeful step toward one's goal, a hand on the head or a pat on the back with blessing one's ministry of love. In this manner we compile a list of ways touch figures significantly in our lives to make us more whole. The combination of skills it takes to know why, when, and how to touch in a manner appropriate to healing process I call heart/hand coordination.

Heart/Hand Coordination

Heart/hand coordination is the human capacity to cooperate with God by communicating the heart's compassion through touch that facilitates healing process.[19] It is different from eye/

hand coordination, which—in medical settings, for example— could refer to the surgeon's manual skills for repairing or curing. In fact, the word "surgeon" evolved from two Greek words which mean "hand's work," emphasizing technical ability. In distinction, heart/hand coordination refers to touch, which enhances energies and processes involving the whole person. Thus, healing touch shaped by heart/hand coordination could help someone experience emotional or spiritual wholeness even when the person is unlikely to find curing for particular physical problems.

Heart/hand coordination unfolds in human development much like the mother archetype discussed by Anthony Stevens, a London psychiatrist who researches mother-infant bonding. According to Stevens the capacity to nurture is built into human beings and expresses itself primarily in terms of "play, physical contact, and social interaction," even more so than the provision of food.[20] The important point Stevens stresses is that the development of archetypal mothering behavior depends on interaction with the infant. Similarly, just as the baby's cry or smile activates nurturing instincts within the parent, behavioral signals also stimulate compassion in the human heart. Once activated, this energy seeks some form of touch as one of its natural expressions. No one taught our three-year-old daughter, Leigh, to place a handful of sopping wet tissue on her mother's sore eyes. When she saw her mom leave the kitchen to lie down and rub her eyes, Leigh acted on her own, coordinating her hands with compassion triggered by the need she accurately perceived.

As a person grows, heart/hand coordination develops naturally, as do other capacities, such as the ability to act morally or to perform cognitive tasks. When I ask college students in workshops to imagine how they would express compassion, they describe themselves as reaching out to touch. Mother Teresa of Calcutta is a model of well-integrated heart/hand coordination.

Heart/hand coordination is routinely suppressed in our culture in favor of other capacities more useful to technological values—such as eye/hand coordination. However, more adults are reclaiming heart/hand coordination, sometimes through their experience of touch in unplanned ways and sometimes in professional bodywork settings such as massage therapy. Listen to two members of the National Association of Bodyworkers in Religious Service tell how heart/hand coordination emerged in their lives.

Pat Reynolds, Sister of Charity, St. Mary's Church, Colts Neck, New Jersey, writes:

> I came into bodywork accidentally. . . . A woman from our parish was dying with cancer and I received a call from her husband asking me to meet him at the hospital. When I did I found her hemorrhaging and crying for help. Because of a nurses' strike I ended up physically caring for her, and I realized I loved doing so. . . .
>
> I believe many are "skin hungry" and are afraid to admit it. Massage can help fill that hunger. Jesus constantly touched, as is so often revealed to us in the Gospels. Massage can be a way to make that touch more real and to let others experience compassion and healing.[21]

Jackie Kingsbury, Zephyrhills, Florida, reports:

> It is said that she who needs it the most will be attracted to bodywork because through personal experience she knows the transformative power possible when one "comes home to herself, her body-spirit." . . .
>
> This ministry is a call to walk with another with deep-seated trust that it is [God's] wisdom guiding the movements within; [the receiver's] is the inner healer. What we can do is be present through our hands, our beings, open to allow a presence larger than us to meet the one receiving massage. . . .
>
> This work is teaching me a deepening sensitivity and presence, a trusting of my intuition . . . letting go of control and thinking I "have to do something" and the ego-invested stance of seeing myself as the healer. It is teaching me to honor any given moment of my client's journey, to accept the pain that may manifest as having some meaning in the person's work and not

something I try to make go away, to simply be a caring presence with the person in his or her emotional pain.

I am delighted to have "happened on" a work so suitable to my life at this time.[22]

When Jesus used touch in response to persons presenting physical symptoms, he acted on the basis of compassion, "gut feelings" (Mark 1:41). He often joined his compassion to the faith brought by receivers (Matt. 9:29; Mark 9:23–29). Faith is certainly the appropriate mode for those whose illness threatens their lives and relationships. We read mostly about Jesus' touch in these healing stories.

However, there were many times Jesus touched to nurture hope that comes from feeling more closely connected in community. We have seen that parents brought children for him to touch (Mark 10:13). Often calling his disciples children (Mark 10:24; John 21:5), Jesus used touch to calm his disciples as though they were children and to replace their fear with a vision of hope (Matt. 17:7).

Then, to encourage servant love, Jesus washed the disciples' feet (John 13:1–20). In addition to supporting his disciples, this touch, like the Last Supper of which it was a part, seemed designed as a ritual for teaching and communicating.

By following Jesus' example, we learn how healing touch originates (*intention*), what it communicates and accomplishes (*expectation*), and that it seeks appropriate occasions for expression (*setting*). These are the main components of heart/hand coordination that form the dynamics of compassionate touch. We will discuss them further in Part 2.

Conclusion

This chapter gives a working vocabulary for healing touch. Using the meanings associated with these terms, we may speak of any instance of human touch or touch skills as an expression of *heart/hand coordination,* as long as it facilitates *healing process* that aims toward *health and wholeness.* By this language we understand that healing touch is not the sole property of specialists, medical or clerical professionals, but belongs to us all. Like any of the Spirit's gifts, we learn about it best as we use it in loving and caring for one another.

PART 2

Touch in
Modern Ministry

CHAPTER 4

The Intention
of Touch
in Pastoral Care

To reclaim healing touch as a part of pastoral care we need to understand the basic dynamics of heart/hand coordination. These dynamics reside in a combination of the caregiver's *intention,* the mutual *expectations* of those involved in the pastoral interaction, and the choices of *setting* in which healing touch occurs.

In this chapter we will focus on intention. The discussion leads us to an in-depth look at motivations and reasons for healing touch. Chapter 5 will complete the discussion of heart/hand coordination by examining mutual expectations and various settings of healing touch. While intention deals mostly with the inner life, expectation and setting pertain to interpersonal realities of healing touch, including procedures for making referrals to those who use touch professionally.

We will discuss all three of the components of heart/hand coordination in light of a typical episode of pastoral care. The pastoral event will probably be familiar to those who have worked in general hospitals. If not, the lessons from this experience will nonetheless serve as useful principles and guidelines in most any pastoral situation.

Cultural Conditioning and Self-Understanding

Before we begin the case study, we need to pick up the discussion of touch gone wrong from chapter 2. Research on battered women, abused children, and sex in parishes and other forbidden zones gives reason for profound pause whenever we discuss intention in the use of touch, especially by clergy.

We have noted Lebacqz and Barton's conclusion in *Sex in the Parish* that situational factors built into ministry make it more difficult for clergy to read intentions accurately. These researchers also identify addictive patterns that influence intentions: co-dependency that makes one feel totally responsible for the welfare of others, theologies that foster martyr complexes, and personality types who want to please and can't say no.[1]

The authors find that male clergy are more vulnerable to conditioning by these factors. Since women are oppressed by these forces, they are less likely to abuse on the basis of such conditioning. Thus, female clergy would have fewer complications within themselves for discerning clear intentions about touch. The authors also note that since women may draw on mothering behavior that models creative and nonpossessive use of power, their touch would be more likely to encourage growth in the other and not to dominate or control.[2]

Having made these comparisons, Lebacqz and Barton go on to say that gut feelings alone will not suffice for anyone in ministry, male or female. A clear ethical framework is also essential—not the kind that aims solely at the minister's character but one that also addresses the power inequities in social arrangements. However, the authors admit that ethical guidelines are hardly any match for the more powerful determinants of behavior wielded by the culture, including child rearing. Ultimately, "in order to develop healthy patterns of sexual relating in the church, the cultural patterns have to be changed."[3]

Such a coalition of cultural and psychic factors produces in human beings a profound capacity for deceiving ourselves and others when it comes to good intentions. More specifically, in a culture where touch has gone wrong and intentions are suspect, the question arises: Should we touch at all? If so, how can we be sure of our motives?

A good case can be made for a no-touch policy, especially for male clergy. A pastor reported, "Touch is always sexual for me, so I've decided never to use it in ministry." As long as this is his experience, no touch in pastoral situations would be a wise policy. The policy makes further sense in light of the culture's reinforcement of sexual meanings that the pastor associates with touch.

The all-important principle this pastor demonstrates is the effort toward self-knowledge. Truly this is the basic task of those who would offer healing touch. Knowing oneself and one's motives is an ongoing spiritual discipline requiring us to hold in creative tension a great paradox: *We have been called and created for healing touch, and we have been so conditioned by touch gone wrong that our motives are mixed—if not at war—within us.* Here are four hints for embracing these opposites.

First, we need daily to assess ourselves in terms of our own healing journeys. We cannot live in the kind of culture we have been analyzing without suffering serious spiritual and emotional injuries that even now we carry around in our psyches and bodies. The question for those who would follow Jesus to be healers for others is not *whether* we have entered a healing journey or recovery program but *what kind.* We have several choices here, from spiritual friends and guides to twelve-step programs to various church and support groups. Whatever form the healing journey or program takes, we should gain from it a clearer sense of where we are on our own roads to recovery. If we cannot tell where we are coming from, how will we be able to discern where others are and thereby render the touch they need?

Second, if we find that the season we are now experiencing in our lives is best described by "faith behaviors," it is entirely possible and appropriate that we should be seeking to receive healing touch rather than giving it. The time we take to find nurturing for ourselves is just as important as giving ourselves in service to others. Making this kind of assessment is a daily task. Since we never stop changing and healing, we cannot expect our capacity for healing touch to remain constantly in an active, giving mode.

Third, we need to realize that changing our touch behavior, even in small ways, can call forth all kinds of resistances. Whenever we let go of patterns of relating that have been conditioned by the culture's addictions and standards, we can be sure the psyche will find ways to return us to the old behaviors. These old behaviors are the ways we have come to know ourselves. Some of them have served us well and some not so well. Changing any of these behaviors means we will also come to know ourselves and our motives differently. Body and soul learn from each other. Paying attention to the ways we resist the changes presents us with clearer knowledge about ourselves and gives us choices about the changes we really want and are ready for.

Fourth, and last, as we encounter in ourselves all sorts of ways we have learned to serve the cultural standards and have seen the harm even a glance, much less a touch, can cause ourselves and others, we are continually confronted with the question of worth. Are we worth knowing? Is self-knowledge worth the effort? What value is it to learn that the evils outside us are also alive and well inside us? What more than grief, sorrow, and anger can such self-knowledge call forth?

Once a client, using bodywork to deal with depression stemming from childhood abuse, said, "No matter how depressed I may be when I come for my appointment, during massage I always hear my body telling me I'm good." Whether we hear the message of our worth and goodness through the body in particular is not the point. What is crucial is the faith that, somewhere in the muck of ourselves, the diamond of our goodness is discoverable in countless ways. The true miracle is that this goodness is so good it helps bear the trials of finding it. God-given goodness gives us the joy not only to bear the pains of honest self-knowing but to share in community with others, whose suffering is just as profound as ours and whose goodness is just as valuable.

The first quality that Mother Teresa of Calcutta looks for in those who would touch and care for the "poorest of the poor" is not strength, patience, or even faith, hope, and love. It is joy. We might add, it would be the kind of joy that has been found within and shaped by the tears of life, not the result of having been shielded from the pain. A gem called the black star sapphire often comes with a saying: "Light over the darkness is the anti-Christ. Light through the darkness is the Christ."[4] When viewed at the proper angle, a star in the shape of cross can be seen shining out of the blackness of this oval jewel. Just so, as we keep turning ourselves away from the false lights that only bring out the motives to make us anti-self and antisocial, we will find the Christ shining through the darkness within us. Then we know that even the evil we have done, and will do, works together for good along with our best efforts.

In summary, discerning motives for healing touch requires knowing where we are on our healing journeys, listening to our resistances, and claiming our goodness buried beneath the rubbish within ourselves. To undertake this kind of self-knowing is a lifelong task. The resources for this discipline are many: the example of Jesus; our bodies, with their array of emotions and intuitions; ethical guidelines; mentors and those who model the collective wisdom of healing traditions; primary relationships of intimacy, such as our families; congregations in which we experience laying on of hands; and last, but not least, those who would receive our healing touches.

Clarifying Initial Intent

As we shall now see in this case study, many of these resources figure in the ongoing self-knowledge that is necessary to clarify our intention. The following discussion is organized according to the outline on Reflection Sheet No. 2: Touch in a Pastoral Care Event in Appendix A. The reflection sheet can be used to guide you in journaling about a moment in your care for another when touch played a significant role. You might return to reread this chapter and the next after using the reflection sheet in this manner.

OVERVIEW
Describe briefly the pastoral event.
As hospital chaplain I was called to be with the parents of a twenty-four-year-old man injured in an industrial accident.

He died in the emergency room. I was sitting next to his mother in the family room, holding her hand, when the doctor came in to tell the family—mother, father, and two siblings—of their loss. The mother became hysterical, running into the hall and throwing herself against the walls and onto the floor. Other family members also spilled into the hall and wailed loudly. A security guard and a patient representative attended to them while I guided the mother back to the room. She fell on her knees.

I got on my knees too, my body flush beside hers, and put an arm around her shoulder. I helped her lean her upper body on the couch. I rocked her gently. Her grief came in waves, beginning low in the torso and rising to shiver the shoulders. So I assisted this movement of energy, placing my hand at mid-back and walking the heel of my hand upward to the shoulders.

Gradually the wailing would subside. Then another wave would wash over her. The other family members began to hold and rock one another. After forty-five minutes of emotional release, they were able to be shown to their cars to return later for viewing the body.

INTENTION

Describe the intuitions, feelings, and motives out of which your touch emerged.

I sensed in myself both anxiety and compassion upon entering this scene. I felt the adrenaline kick in, preparing me for quick responses. I also felt I was "standin' in the need of prayer," so I sent up my usual short supplication: "Help!" I remember breathing deeply as I held the mother's hand, since I already knew of the death. I'm not sure if, at first, I was holding the mother's hand or she was holding mine. Certainly we were all in it together.

By the end of the episode I felt touch had helped us progress to a calmer center. It really helped me know viscerally, in a way I might not have known otherwise, what the mother was experiencing. I definitely had a gut feeling connected to the touch.

My motives for touching became clearer, actually, as the episode progressed. The mother was being thrown around,

> so to speak, by her waves of grief. The sight of the security
> guard reminded me I had plenty of help. So it wasn't my job
> to restrain her. Rather, my motive became that of staying with
> her in the midst of her mourning, representing as chaplain
> the presence of God in the midst of chaos.

Notice the variety of emotional states, ranging from anxiety, compassion, and gut feelings to togetherness and a sense of presence. Typically, pastoral events churn up a flurry of emotions that register in various places in the body. To clarify our intentions, we need to listen to these churnings. We are more apt to misuse touch or omit it inappropriately if we do not pay attention to these somatic signals.

Hospital volunteers in training sometimes say, "I feel like I just want to reach out and hold the patient." Good! That feeling is God-given. Of course, touching depends on other factors too, as we shall see. But how can we touch if we do not feel moved to do so?

Discerning to Touch or Not

Feeling the desire to touch compassionately is the fundamental energizer of heart/hand coordination. If we are to take Mark 1:41 seriously, healing touch as demonstrated by Jesus originates in strongly felt emotions. Variant readings of this passage contain two words describing Jesus' motivation—anger (*orgisthes*) and compassion (*splanchnisthes*). Since the latter is also used to refer to the heart, we might say that healing touch is touch that is first "heartfelt." Dr. Jules Older, a psychologist who teaches touch to medical students, says, "Touch only when you [genuinely] feel like touching." Otherwise, those you touch "will quickly pick up the contrived touch for what it is, and the result will be greater distrust, not a stronger bond." [5]

Listening for the desire to touch also sharpens the ability to detect the body's signals that warn against touch. Dr. Older continues, "Don't *always* touch when you feel like touching." [6]

In an emergency-room incident similar to the example just

described, I was with the mother and daughter of a family member who had died. Six other family members had wanted a joint meeting with the doctor, but they had been shown to another waiting area. A legal problem connected with the case required the hospital to attend to these parties separately. As the doctor made her report to the mother and daughter, several of the others burst into the room. A heated controversy ensued between them and the doctor. Though I wanted to give the mother a comforting hand on the shoulder, I feared it would amplify the drama of "us versus them." The fright I felt was a clear signal not to touch.

Dr. Older lists five signals not to touch:

1. You don't want to.
2. You sense the patient doesn't want you to.
3. You want to and you sense the patient wants you to, but you do not feel this is the most effective therapeutic maneuver.
4. You feel you're being manipulated, conned, or coerced to touch.
5. You suspect you're going to manipulate, con, or coerce the patient by your touch.[7]

What about situations that are not as clear, when we get mixed signals? During clinical pastoral education I walked into the room of a very attractive twenty-three-year-old patient, Susan. Her roommate had a male visitor. The man kept turning toward Susan and making remarks that interrupted our conversation. Finally, he reached out and sensuously stroked Susan's arm. She recoiled from his touch. Feeling angry and protective, I excused us from his company by pulling the dividing curtain between the beds. Now Susan and I could have the privacy we needed.

I was left with a double message. The man's touch demonstrated what I considered totally inappropriate behavior. But now I wanted to do the same thing. My breathing became constricted. It was unclear to me whether Susan would trust my touch any more than his. Even more to the point was the question whether my motives were any clearer than the man's. I kept the visit touch free.

Situations are apt to be unclear when we cannot distinguish our desire for healing touch from other desires, such as sexual ones. Part of the answer to this problem is a set of clear ethical guidelines. I believe our bodies help us in this regard. In the example just described, I experienced tightening in the chest and constriction of my breathing. These were the body's signals that I was not centered.

In her book *Reclaiming Healthy Sexual Energy*, psychologist Anne Stirling Hastings tells how to discern healthy sexual energy from unhealthy cross-wired motives. By substituting the word "compassion" for "sexual energy" in her instructions, we have excellent advice on listening to the body's ethical guidelines regarding our intention for touching.

1. Is this compassion emerging gently out of my spiritual center? Or is it grabbing me, stimulated from outside myself?
2. Is the compassion I feel three-dimensional, filling and flooding me, enhancing all my other feelings? Or is it of one-dimensional intensity that can prevent me from having other feelings?
3. Do I feel warmly relaxed, breathing easily and fully, as I welcome compassion? Or do I feel tensed up, muscles hard and tight, and breathing hard with arousal?[8]

An important aside here is that healthy sexual touch can and should be healing touch when all the factors in heart/hand coordination are properly integrated for the purpose of sexual behavior. When the goals are pastoral, and then sexual intentions enter the scene, the body registers this cross-wiring and sends the kind of ethical warning signals Hastings describes.

David Calof, internationally respected authority on treating survivors of incest and childhood abuse, says that if he experiences sexual attraction during therapy with a female client, he will not use touch with that client.[9] Deldon Anne McNeely, a Jungian analyst, writes in *Touching: Body Therapy and Depth*

Psychology that touch "motivated by the analyst's need for gratification is *never* justified, and when it is done amounts to exploitation of the patient."[10]

These authorities emphasize the ethical aspect of intention. To be healing, touch must intend to serve the healing process, not the toucher's needs. Heeding our body's signals and intuitions should not set us at cross-purposes with our fundamental commitment to be healers in moments of pastoral care. McNeely says our "most significant tools are personal body awareness as well as intuition and a clear ethical stance."[11]

Thus in the thick of pastoral encounters we need to balance a conscious vocational identity with an awareness of our body and intuition. It is easier to do this if we have taken seriously our ongoing need to develop better body awareness and intuitive skills. Giving and receiving massage therapy has been, for me, a laboratory for that kind of personal growth. In addition, I must remind myself of the larger commitment to be a servant of the healing process. How do we keep that larger intent in focus?

Spiritual Guidance for Touch

Notice in the journal of the pastoral event that I sent up my usual short prayer, "Help!" (I often think of this prayer as a mini-version of the African-American petition, "Lord, help me find a way where there is no way!") Then I took several deep breaths. I call these exercises "prayers on the run." They help me keep the proper frame of mind.

In addition to these prayers in process, every morning I use a brief ritual that frames the day in light of the petition for God's help. I light a stick of incense, which gives off a pleasant scent. I walk with it around my therapy room, lifting up in prayer the clients I will see that day and concluding with the Lord's Prayer. Then I take the stick outside as a symbol of connection between the therapy, the creation, and the Creator.

Psychoanalyst and professor of psychology and religion Robert L. Moore defines prayer as "any means by which we make contact with the energy of divine reality and which reminds us that we are not the Creator."[12] Each person will have his or her unique way of contacting the central vision of shalom or the divine energy for help. Lobsang Rapgay, a physician to the Dalai Lama, told me he always calls on the Medicine Buddha before he touches a patient. Therapist Dolores Krieger teaches her students of "therapeutic touch" first to center themselves in order to clarify their motives. Christians, too, will have many ways we put our hands "in the hand of the man from Galilee": prayers of dedication, visualizations of shalom, moments of centering meditation, deep-breathing exercises, conversing with a spiritual friend or counselor. A powerful motivator is regular receiving, giving, or witnessing healing touch in liturgies of laying on of hands for health and wholeness.

As we saw in chapter 3, we simultaneously remember and envision health and wholeness. The inspiration of shalom both energizes the healer and drives the healing process. Getting in touch with that spiritual resource vitalizes and orients our basic intentions.

Conclusion

Intention is, perhaps, the most important component of heart/hand coordination. Mirka Knaster, cross-cultural researcher of bodywork, says that "technique itself does not seem to matter as much as . . . the intent of the person touching. That's where the element of compassion enters."[13] Even when touch is not used, one's intention can have therapeutic effect. Studies of various psychotherapies find that what makes them effective is not the specific technique but the therapist's intentions of warmth and unconditional regard.[14] Qi Gong healers in China have for centuries mastered the art of intentionally directing their energy for healing purposes without directly touching.[15] Research of gifted healers such as the Methodist lay leader Olga Worrell is often designed to study this factor. In experiments conducted in 1979–1981, containers of a bacterial system were placed in her hands and in the hands of a "naive" healer (one lacking any established healing abilities and un-aware of the purpose of the experiment). The purpose was to see whether or not either healer would be able to extend the lifespan of the bacteria when a solution was added that nor-mally inhibits their growth. After four hours, 121 percent more bacteria survived in Worrell's hands than in the container held by the other person. In fact, no effect was detected in the bacte-ria held by this person. The experiment was replicated a year later.[16]

I have never felt called to become a healer as defined by these energetic traditions. But I do think we have a great deal to learn from Olga Worrell and others about the importance of intent. Insofar as all Christians are called to serve healing pro-cesses, this underlying calling transforms our intentions. I have found that reflecting on my own touch behavior is an excellent way to work on my intention. The more I do this, the clearer I become regarding my limits and abilities with touch.

Early in my bodywork practice I believed there was an un-limited amount of good I could accomplish through my hands. I thought I could comfort those with the deepest depressions and the most bizarre backgrounds of abuse. With this attitude I did not realize how dependent I was on my clients and their improvement. As with any co-dependency, the issue that keeps surfacing is that of control. The self-knowledge I needed is the lesson anyone must learn who wants to carry out the commis-sion to heal: There are limits to what we can control. Gerald G. May confesses for all of us when he says he had been "trying to command the very process of healing."[17]

Now I am much less ambitious about what I can do through touch. Being centered and confident in God's control of the healing process should always take priority over what I might expect to accomplish with my hands. I learned about this inter-play between intention and expectation in a bodywork session I provided for a survivor of incest. I had been using several tech-niques to help the client get in touch with images and memories furnished by her body. None of the techniques was doing what

I had hoped. Instead, she became more anxious. Finally, I stopped and rested my hand on the middle of her back while we both took deep breaths for a few minutes. This moment of reconnecting to our centers proved to be a memorable one for the client, who described the touch as warm and providing security. After this session, the client began to think of bodywork, which she had initially feared, as a safe place to be.

When I am tempted to expect touch to accomplish too much, events like this remind me of the ongoing importance of continually focusing the intent, reconnecting to the center, and offering up what I do to serve more than my own need to control. Not my will, but thine.

CHAPTER 5

Expectations and Settings of Touch

Whenever touch is used in a pastoral encounter, both parties consciously and unconsciously are taking note of whether the touch fits their expectations about the pastoral interaction and whether it is appropriate to the setting. If we want touch to stay within the bounds of mutually agreeable expectations, we will be sensitive to the timing of touch and whether it clearly supports pastoral objectives.

First, we demonstrate sensitivity to timing when we (1) assess accurately the phase of healing process that a receiver is experiencing, (2) identify any signals of resistance within ourselves or the receiver, and (3) hear the receiver's permission to touch. These aspects of timing alert us to where we are, so we can be clearer about where we are going if we use touch.

Second, it is helpful to state specific pastoral objectives for touch—and likewise for no touch. Caregivers rarely take time to do so, accustomed as we are to remaining unaware of our touch behavior. However, since most of our touches are probably more effective than we realize, the effort to articulate what good they can do only strengthens the clarity of our overall pastoral goals. Furthermore, such awareness of touch behavior is an excellent check to ensure proper boundaries, alerting us to unconscious ways we may be intruding or isolating ourselves interpersonally.

Part of this effort toward greater clarity about objectives of touch is to discern whether the touch we think is needed is in fact appropriate to traditional pastoral settings. If not, perhaps the receiver may benefit from proper referral to another setting, such as provided by those who offer professional touch therapy. In this manner the issue of setting, the final component of heart/

hand coordination, unfolds naturally out of our discussion of expectation.

The issue of setting arises with particular urgency in our day as a result of the modern bodywork movement. We now have many options for referring people to touch therapists—perhaps too many. Besides the ever-increasing specializations in Western medicine, the burgeoning holistic alternatives of faith healers, New Age gurus, and bodywork gimmicks boggle the mind. Many of the marketed forms of touch come wrapped in garb (metaphysical or otherwise) totally foreign to the Western psyche. While these diverse offerings have a strong appeal, they sometimes show mindless disregard of basic therapeutic principles.

Though bodywork is no different from any profession in having to weed out those who would make specious claims for their work, the reemergence of these ancient healing arts in our day is basically positive. It presents us with choices we did not have just two decades ago. We should not ignore these options. If we do, we may not be helping ourselves and others as effectively as we might to find the setting for the kind of touch that best enables us to heal.

Ironically, the most overlooked setting for healing touch is worship. Intentions and expectations of healing touch in worship are so muddled that we need to take a much closer look at this setting, which we will do in chapter 6.

Let us begin our focus on expectation and setting as the remaining two components of heart/hand coordination. We will continue using Reflection Sheet No. 2 in Appendix A, with which we began the case study in chapter 4.

EXPECTATIONS

Describe the receiver's situation.

I knew the family's situation would be that of initial shock over the loss of a loved one. So, upon entering, I sat with the mother. When the doctor arrived, I sensed fear rising in everyone, especially the mother. She extended her hands to either side of her for support. I held one of her hands while the husband held the other. At this moment touch communicated courage for facing the test they correctly suspected was upon them.

Timing

A basic issue that arises regarding whether one touches (and, if so, the form of touch) is the phase of healing the receiver is experiencing. In the emergency room I used hand holding, back and shoulder supporting with both arms and hands, and rocking against the side of my body. These methods are common in acute hospital settings in which pastoral care is provided in the initial grief stages of healing process.

However, when I served as chaplain in a physical rehabilitation hospital, touch tended to take different forms. Here the patients had already experienced the more dramatic tests of faith. In rehab they faced the longer road to hope, putting the pieces of their lives back together. Much of my pastoral care had to do with helping them celebrate the daily gains that graced their lives. New muscle action, for example, no matter how small, was often a stroke patient's sign of hope both physically and spiritually. In these cases we often shared the good news with a high five or a brief embrace of the affected area to welcome the part back into the whole.

The form of touch changed once again in relation to outpatients, many of whom returned as hospital volunteers. A wheelchair athlete who counsels quadriplegics told me he liked the encouraging squeeze on his arm or shoulder I would give him. He said he could always tell where people were coming from by their touch; too many of them, he complained, conveyed a pitying message. Those giving such a message by their touch apparently allowed the wheelchair to obscure a true reading of the athlete's healing journey.

Taking the receiver's phase of recovery into consideration, the first factor in our decision to touch and in shaping kinds of touch, is called *assessment*. Touch is hardly healing if it ignores the fact that the same therapeutic maneuver can have dramatically different meanings and effects depending on the receiver's situation.

If there is some question about the appropriateness of touch in a particular instance, the giver may not have a clear sense of where the receiver is in the healing process. Further assessment is required. Several additional factors could also be involved.

Describe how touch became part of the pastoral episode.

Upon hearing the bad news, the family literally attempted to run from it. They were beside themselves. I remember resisting the impulse to restrain the mother by my grip. Instead, I wanted my hands to communicate strength in the presence of death. I helped her off the floor and held her against the side of my body. This helped bring her back into her skin. The situation necessitated that my touch be firm to offer stability within the chaos of her feelings.

The second factor that affects whether, when, and how touch enters a pastoral event is the giver's sense of *resistance* within himself or herself and within the receiver. In this hospital episode, my resistance to restraining the mother kept me from playing the role of security guard or some other staff person whose job it is to provide safety for patients and employees. Resistances to touch are body signals equally as significant as heartfelt feelings for touch. Heeding both messages is part of the work of compassion. By paying attention to one's resistances, opportunities arise to gain a better understanding of one's motives, a clearer picture of the receiver's situation, and a firmer sense of the dynamics of the helping relationship.[1]

Awareness of one's resistances also heightens sensitivity to resistances in the receiver. In visiting a patient who was a survivor of a particularly cruel history of abuse, I sensed her uncertainty. During the visit a nurse entered to give the patient a long and painful injection. I held out my hand to offer support, asking, "Would you like to hold on?" She pulled her arm away as if to say, I can go it alone. While respecting her wishes not to be touched, I remained by her side. During the treatment the patient changed her mind and reached out to take my hand. Later, in the hospital chapel, she came to receive her first communion. Apparently, she perceived the touch as meaning an opportunity to draw nearer to God. I believe this outcome might not have occurred had a healing touch not been available.

A third issue in timing is the *invitation,* or permission to touch. Clearing up uncertainty in timing is often simply a matter of paying attention to the receiver's signals for touch. These can be verbal or nonverbal requests, as in the hospital episode when the mother reached out for support. When these signals are not clear, I ask, for example, "Would you like to join hands as we pray?" However, I don't always touch on the basis of the receiver's invitation. Some persons compulsively invite touch because it perpetuates their self-understanding as one without boundaries. It is not uncommon for survivors of physical or sexual abuse to display this behavior. Respectfully *not* touching or limiting touch in response to people in these life situations may be the most healing response.

In summary, caregivers can expect that their touch will emerge in pastoral encounters in a timely manner if they have made accurate assessment of the receiver's phase of healing, have honored resistances in themselves and in receivers, and have heard an invitation or permission to touch.

Pastoral Objectives of Touch

Describe the effects of your touch.

> By touch I learned something of the nature of the mother's experience. I felt the powerful surges of her grief. This information, along with the sight of the security guard, helped remind me of my role as a bringer of pastoral presence rather than restraint. I remember the moment this clarity occurred, for I loosened my grip around her shoulders, giving her more breathing room. Then the goal of my touch was more consciously to affirm her feelings and to give them a safe place to be expressed.
>
> That this message got through was indicated by a gradual

return to a calmer center and by the fact that the other family members, not touching at first, were given permission to hold and comfort one another.

In addition to touch entering pastoral care episodes in a timely manner, expectation as a component of heart/hand coordination also has to do with touch helping to accomplish pastoral goals. In the journal of the emergency room incident, the goals or objectives were fairly immediate: to protest against feeling overwhelmed by fear, to strengthen the connection between body and psyche, and to provide a safe environment for the expression of grief. Touch was my primary pastoral resource to reach these goals.

Given proper timing, touch may assist you toward several pastoral objectives. Here are five basic ones that occur frequently with those involved in healing ministry.

First, *to complement interpersonal rituals.* Handshakes, hugs, and pats on the back create friendly relational space. As Mother Theresa makes her way among the poorest of the poor and among her co-workers, she brings peace and courage through her hands, constantly welcoming, encouraging, and blessing. If we knew the true desperation of most of those we encounter every day, we might find ourselves using touch more often in our daily rituals.

Second, *to assist the mechanics of communication.* A hand respectfully but seriously placed on the shoulder for a few seconds can prepare a person to receive a message. Briefly supporting the person's upper arm also holds his or her attention and can add emphasis to what we are saying. With couples or groups, placing one's hand momentarily against a knee with palm outward and fingers upward, as if stopping traffic, can signal a halt to excessive verbiage from one person so others may proceed to express themselves. These uses of touch are meant to assist communication. As Dr. Older reminds us, "Touch is an adjunct to—not a substitute for—talking and listening." [2]

Third, *to add depth to conversation.* With those in the long haul of recovery processes, a brief stimulating squeeze of the upper arm or shoulder as you walk or talk can make it easier to bear sorrow, fear, or panic. With those in grief, an arm around the shoulder or upper back often reaches deeper than words ever will. In prayer, taking the hand of someone with AIDS or someone with mental or behavioral problems brings the "untouchables" once again into relationship with the larger body of Christ.

Fourth, *to model healthy behavior.* In working with families who have learned to fear one another because physical or emotional boundaries have been transgressed, respectful treatment of their bodily presence, through touch or no touch, teaches healthier behavior. Many times I have found such families huddled in a corner away from the loved one who is dying. Placing my hands on the patient breaks the spell of fear and gives the family permission to come over to touch and say good-bye. In liturgies of healing, those who witness laying on of hands are often just as moved as those who receive it. Given the skin hunger we develop in our culture from no touch, and given our proclivity to homophobia, adult males who express affectionate touch with younger children, and especially with boys, contribute a truly healing touch in our society. The point here is that the mere sight of healthy touch can trigger more wholesome options for those who witness it.

The same principle applies in families who learn healing arts such as massage. I find that the verbal skills necessary for couples to learn massage are also fundamental to nurturing healthy relationships. They must practice articulating what they want, being willing to receive as well as give, listening accurately, offering nonjudgmental feedback, and expressing a sense of creativity and play. Healing arts in families model health on many levels.

Fifth, *to enhance inner exploration and reflection.* Once during a hospital visit I took the hand of an elderly woman near death. Conversation stopped, but she continued looking at our hands clasped together. She turned them this way and that, examining every angle in silence for several minutes. I asked, "Are you doing OK?" She said, "Yes, I'm just remembering." The sustained contemplation of joined hands was for this woman a key that opened the door to an inner life rich with memories and feelings.[3]

Referrals

The benefits of touch for inner exploration point us to a major reason for the growing popularity of professional bodywork. Many bodyworkers have discovered how touch will trigger the memory of a past event. In one of my clients the memory was an attempted sexual abuse. I asked what it was like for a man to touch her with a different intention. She said, "It's healing." In another case I noticed that the woman held her shoulder stiff as if she were fending me off. I asked her if she had ever been injured or abused there. She said she had not. A year later I received a letter from her saying that her shoulder did indeed carry the memory of an abusive event which she had just then been able to recall.

As more therapists become familiar with body memory, they find ways to listen to the body talk. Deldon Anne McNeely introduced touch in her work because her "expectation was that direct body touch would . . . open [clients] more to feeling responses by contacting energy that could not be reached by verbal methods."[4]

Introducing formal touch therapies to gain access to unconscious content stored in the body requires much skill and training. It often requires special settings for professional bodywork, which differ from those associated with the roles of clergy and with most traditional helping professionals. An organization of body-oriented psychotherapy is emerging, and some religious professionals are using touch therapies as part of their ministry.[5] However, we need to remember that the vast majority of today's clients do not expect to receive touch therapy as part of the services provided by religious and other helping professionals in traditional settings.

Given this reality, when the need for professional touch

arises, the necessity for making good referrals becomes apparent. Here is an example of how that need might arise.

A pastoral counselor had worked for several months with a young man on issues of self-esteem. The client would often say, "I have trouble standing up to my parents (or teachers, etc.)." Also, his drinking problem had caused him to fall on several occasions, resulting in serious injuries. The counselor thought better body awareness was an important part of the man's recovery, so he referred the client to me for massage therapy. I worked primarily on his legs. After the third session he said, "Hey! I'm standing up better." Immediately, the client connected his standing up better with his "standing up to" significant people in his life. He saw how his issues with authority were almost literally translating themselves into physical behavior. Later he would take these centered feelings gained from bodywork as a resource for more self-confidence in relationships with authority figures.

The next section, on Setting, contains more examples of how professional bodywork can be part of the healing process. The point here is that recognizing the need for formal professional touch and making good referrals are basic functions of healthy expectations in heart/hand coordination.

In referring people to bodywork professionals for touch therapies, five steps should be considered.

1. *Research the bodyworker* to whom you may refer your client. The best way is to experience the work yourself. Are you left with a feeling that you want to return? Have your physical, emotional, and spiritual boundaries been respected? Is the bodyworker agreeable to consultation regarding your client? What are his or her experience, credentials, and recommendations from others? If you are referring a person with a background of physical or sexual abuse, it is imperative to ascertain the level of training and experience the bodyworker has in this field.

2. *Give clear reasons to your client* why you are making the referral. Do not treat the referral as a prescription to be filled. Enlist the client's participation in clarifying what he or she wants from the experience.

3. *Recommend a series of bodywork sessions.* Clients spend a great deal of energy in the first session or two getting used to the bodyworker, the setting, and the processes of therapy. Referrals to bodywork therapy as an adjunct to counseling are rarely useful as a one-shot treatment.

4. *Help integrate the bodywork experience* in relation to the pastoral goals for the client. The point is not to evaluate the bodyworker but to hear what the bodywork produced—feelings, memories, visions, or unexpected experiences such as dissociation, tears, or other effects. A conversation with or report from the bodyworker is helpful. Respect the guidelines of confidentiality. Keep in mind that the *process* of listening to and through the body is as important as the *content* that emerges from the bodywork. This step is also important to reinforce the counselor's role as the main representative or caretaker of the therapeutic relationship. In other words, no referral should imply that the counselor is unloading his or her client on someone else.

5. *Seek consultation* if there is any question regarding timing or possible physical or emotional barriers. Enthusiasm for bodywork is fine, but it should not obscure obvious contraindications.

In making appropriate referrals for professional touch therapies, counselors are not only clarifying expectations but are also showing sensitivity to the third ingredient in heart/hand coordination—setting.

SETTINGS

Thus far in our discussion of touch in pastoral care we have made reference to three settings—traditional, professional bodywork, and liturgical. The journal of the pastoral event we are following is a description of healing touch in a traditional setting—hospital chaplaincy. We will conclude this case study with comments on setting guided by the last section of Reflection Sheet No. 2.

Describe the setting of this episode.

The waiting room was set apart from more public areas. Ancillary staff (security guard, patient representative) were present and experienced in working with families in crisis. The physical arrangement (furniture, rug, lamps, similar to a home living room) provided the kind of container the family needed to be themselves in this moment. It also made healing touch a natural resource for pastoral presence.

I noticed that in the brief prayer I gave before leaving, none of the family members "undid" themselves from the supportive holding and touching they were using.

The form of healing touch in this case study is informal in the sense that it is part of a traditional pastoral setting that is characterized mainly by verbal and emotional means of interaction. There are many other examples of traditional settings in which touch can be expected to be an informal part of the scene: pastoral visits in various institutions caring for inpatients, visitation in homes and funeral establishments, counseling in pastoral care centers or churches, and counseling in many agencies that bring services to those who are healing.

However, when a pastoral objective calls for the interaction to be carried out *primarily* by touch (for example, using bodywork to gain a more direct access to memory or feeling), a shift has been made to a formal method of healing touch. Any formal use of healing touch means the giver has received special training, uses specific kinds of preparations and procedures, and may use specially designed equipment and space. Formal touch requires settings different from settings we associate with informal touch.

The remainder of this chapter concerns the setting in which formal touch is used by professional bodyworkers.

Paradigms of Professional Bodywork

Knowledge of modern bodywork is crucial if proper use of and referrals to professionals in these settings are to be made.

There is now such a demand for bodywork that many different methods are available. Not all bodywork disciplines have created professional standards of practice and systems of accountability. Fortunately, leaders of major bodywork schools and professional bodywork organizations are now engaged in serious discussion about scope of practice, referring to issues of professional and ethical boundaries and appropriate settings.

Sources for descriptions of the most popular methods of bodywork are included in the Bibliography and Resources. Rather than produce yet another inventory here, it is more to the point to ask how one determines what type of bodywork is most useful for a particular phase of healing process.

In this inquiry, we are greatly assisted by bodyworkers' perceptions of their own profession. Beginning in May 1990, a Job Analysis Committee of the American Massage Therapy Association (AMTA) began study of about one hundred types of hands-on practice. By the summer of 1991 several members of this committee published an article in *Massage Therapy Journal* to help the growing bodywork profession gain an accurate understanding of its scope of practice. The authors reported that "in essence three fundamental mutually inclusive and interrelated paradigms . . . underlie all forms of massage/bodywork."[6] They also determined that each paradigm, or model, called for a certain level of expertise. The least training was required to provide bodywork for *relaxation*. An added level of ability was necessary to evaluate and apply corrective techniques for *remedial* purposes. Finally, a panoply of psychological, energetic, and bodywork skills were needed to direct a *holistic* approach.

Rather than focusing on the therapist's level of training, I find these models more useful as descriptions of different purposes. Thus, any bodywork style would fall into one of three basic categories according to whether it aimed to be relaxing, integrating, or repairing. (If we change the order of the second and third categories, the sequence will correlate directly with the main purposes of the phases of the threefold healing process.) Let's examine how each model addresses a particular phase.

Relaxing bodywork is described as a nurturing, caring touch that is "noninvasive, relaxing, pleasurable, sensual but not sexual, and stress-reducing."[7] Most graduates of Western massage schools provide this kind of bodywork, generally known as Swedish massage. It is characterized by the application of oil in long flowing strokes and by kneading and other techniques to relax specific muscle groups and provide nurturance through the skin. Such massage therapists often work in private settings and use relaxing music, hot or cold packs as needed, and possibly hydrotherapy. They may apply gentle rocking techniques and quiet cradling for balancing energies. They may also attend to specific aches and pains through deep-tissue work, stretching, and sports massage. However, in general their primary purpose is to help the person relax, release tensions, and benefit from healthier circulation of body fluids and energies.

This model offers the kinds of setting that appropriately address the needs of persons in the early phases of healing process. Those "faithing it" need to be held, to let go, and to release stress, fear, and grief, which are so often locked tight in the muscles. I have found many times that persons coming for massage have already done the most important faith work by simply making the decision to put themselves in someone's else's hands.

In the second model, bodywork for *integrating* the whole person "focuses on how the healing, evolution, and growth of the body/mind/spirit of the individual is enhanced in an integrated way."[8] While relaxing bodywork provides settings for release, integrated approaches combine bodywork, movement, and other activities for gathering the person together again. The purpose is to enable persons to sense some movement through their difficulties and to work with their problems as "opportunities . . . to seek a higher order of function and well-being."[9]

By enabling someone to pick up life's pieces and recover from various problems for greater wholeness, integrated approaches encourage the broad middle phase we call hope. Body-oriented psychotherapies come in many styles and labels. It is a safe generalization that no one style dominates the field as an authoritative standard. Rather, some basic principles—

such as the body's capacity to remember and to express hidden stories through its symptoms, shapes, and movements—are adapted by practitioners to methods they design out of their creative and intuitive faculties.

Psychosynthesis, begun by Roberto Assagioli, makes use of Gestalt therapy as practiced, for example, by Fritz Perls. It is not a form of bodywork as such; rather, it is a psychotherapy open to utilizing a variety of methods to enable the client to hear and integrate the body's signals. Tensions, gestures, and images emerging from dreams and meditation are amplified in active, imaginative ways—journal keeping, guided imagery, movement, symbolic art work, dance, and bodywork. In recent years leaders in psychosynthesis have drawn from the techniques of focusing, as developed by psychologist Eugene Gendlin. They use methods and metaphors that connect mind and body, bringing about a synthesis that enables clients to pay attention to the body's "felt sense" of a particular problem or concern. The goals of psychosynthesis are to help people sift through their many "sub-personalities," to develop intuition of a higher or a larger self, and to use their wills in order to make more creative choices for their lives.[10]

While psychosynthesis incorporates body-awareness techniques into a theory of psychotherapy, other forms of therapy may work from the opposite direction. Somatosynthesis, developed by Clyde Ford, works basically with the body and uses psychotherapeutic insights as they may apply. Ford begins with the capacity of the unconscious, when the body is in a relaxed state, to furnish images and metaphors useful to working one's way along a "healing journey." Somatosynthesis is an excellent example of how a bodywork therapist uses touch to facilitate rather than control healing process.[11]

Body-oriented psychotherapists have great respect for the myriad ways our lives become fragmented. We are often broken into many pieces, but our brokenness harbors the hope that we might be reknit stronger than before—a phenomenon Malcolm Brown calls "creative disorganization."[12] Therapists such as Brown may help us become aware of how the parts can be more creatively reunited to the whole—the essence of hope behavior.

Finally, a third model refers to all forms of bodywork that deal with the immediate causes and consequences of muscular aches and pains in order to assist the body in repairing itself. Unlike the integrating methods, which lead one through a journey for reconnecting many selves and parts, *remedial* bodywork says, "So you've got tension in your neck; let's work it out." This kind of bodywork is like a cup of water for a parched throat. It is handy for the wear and tear that comes simply from carrying out the demands of right livelihood. Receiving regular professional attention for the body's aches and pains before they get worse demonstrates how one can be loving toward oneself.

Muscular pain that stems from old injuries, emotional tension, repetitive motion, or from holding one's posture for prolonged periods of time (dentists, musicians, computer operators, bedridden patients) is not usually addressed in traditional health care settings except by prescription of muscle relaxants. Body awareness gained from massage therapy helped me recognize this fact. As hospital chaplain for twelve years, I noticed that patients who complained about muscle soreness would often say that no medical professional had ever touched or examined the sore muscle.

Janet G. Travell, emeritus clinical professor of medicine at the George Washington University School of Medicine, made a similar observation early in her medical career. She was told that the cause of muscle pain in the hospital's pulmonary patients was reflex from the lung or, in cardiac patients, reflex from the heart. She also saw how the cause of secretaries' muscle pain was often reported as psychosomatic. Travell thought it odd that such explanations were given when "the skeletal muscles had not been examined."[13] Upon her own examination through touch, Travell found that patients with pain complaints had "isolated tender spots in muscle which when compressed reproduced the patient's pain. . . . The common ailment was an unrecognized myofascial trigger-point syndrome."[14] On the basis of Travell's work and that of her associate, David G. Simons, methods are now available using touch to deal effectively with common muscle soreness.[15]

Many other remedial methods also attend directly to correcting musculoskeletal imbalances. Bodywork as developed by Ida P. Rolf stretches connective tissue (fascia) between muscle and bone to allow greater ease in movement and more balanced posture.[16] Several Eastern methods are very useful for energizing tired bodies. The vibrational techniques of Chinese massage (*tuina*), the pressure of Japanese bodywork (*amma* and *shiatsu*), and the stretching and bending of traditional Thai massage (*nuad bo-rarn*) all have in common the intent to stimulate energy flow for correcting specific ailments. If you get weary of doing good and the causes of love and justice drain, burn, and bend you out of shape, the healing touch you need may be found in a variety of bodywork methods that assist the body's efforts to repair itself.

In these ways we see how the major paradigms of bodywork address the themes inherent in the phases of the threefold healing process. However, we need not make these correlations according to a rigid formula. Exceptions will inevitably arise as we make decisions in individual cases. (For example, some who are just beginning to heal may need something other than a referral to a relaxing setting.) Rather, this discussion emphasizes that we do have choices when it comes to using professional bodywork as healing touch. These choices should include at the very least a consideration of the receiver's phase of healing and an informed assessment of the kinds of approaches now available in the setting of professional bodywork that best address the life situation of the receiver.

Setting and Ethics

A disregard for the importance of setting will result in unwise use of bodywork. When I was a hospital chaplain I once gave a neck massage to a man who had been hospitalized on his back for several weeks. I felt compassion (intent). Both the patient and I were sure of the goals (expectation). But I could have been fired. The massage therapist I was becoming jumped into territory belonging to the traditional hospital chaplain I had been hired to be. This incident helped me become aware that the kind of healing touch I really wanted to provide, and which was genuinely needed, called for a different setting. A year later I moved from the hospital setting to work in facilities appropriate for professional bodywork.

We are living in a time when a variety of therapy methods are being combined and tested. It is inevitable that settings may sometimes be superimposed or conflated, especially those contained in the integrating paradigm. Questions about effectiveness and ethics must constantly be raised.

While applauding innovative approaches that integrate professional touch skills (such as massage), psychological and pastoral authorities emphasize the importance of keeping roles distinct and within their appropriate settings. They see no danger in anyone's learning healing arts and using them for family and friends. They do see a problem if someone without the proper credentials should charge fees for such healing. Finally, to dramatize the issues, if clergy or others in traditional counseling settings and roles should personally make formal touch skills available (for example, pastors making appointments to massage parishioners), we would have "clear boundary violation"—in the words of one authority who works with clergy who abuse. Thus, we see the importance of setting. To ignore these issues, caregivers, especially clergy, risk confusing their roles as well as those they intend to serve.

Bruce Nelson is a psychotherapist who has received training from David Calof, an internationally respected authority on working with survivors of abuse. Nelson has also studied massage therapy and is convinced that bodywork is crucial in recovery programs. However, he does not combine these disciplines in his own practice but refers clients for bodywork when timing is right. To his mind, the idea of providing his own clients a combination of counseling plus massage runs several risks. It could replay with negative consequences, for example, the role confusion experienced in childhood by a client whose parent was at once caregiver, lover, and brutal disciplinarian. It could also suffocate the healing process, in his opinion, by applying a nurturing presence so closely that the client does not have the needed psychic space to deal with anger.

Until we offer more comprehensive training programs and establish centers whose setting clearly supports integrated approaches utilizing touch, we would do well to develop models in which professionals coordinate their specialities on behalf of clients. Such a "psychophysical model" is being used by Atlanta-based psychologist Robert J. Timms and massage therapist Patrick Connors. Together these professionals enable clients to take full advantage of a setting in which touch elicits memories and feelings necessary for healing yet protects clients from the risks run by role and boundary diffusion.[17]

CONCLUSION

Those in caregiving roles who use healing touch or recommend professional touch need to become sensitive to all three components of heart/hand coordination. *Focused intention* helps us to be fully present with others whether we touch or not. If touch is appropriate, *clear expectations* make our touch timely and pastorally effective. Choosing *proper settings* enables us to make wise use of our roles, as well as of other professional resources for healing touch. As we pay attention to all these dynamics, heart/hand coordination will become integrated in our lives and thus be expressed in more compassionate and faithful healing ministries.

CHAPTER 6

Healing Touch
in Worship

When I first noticed that almost all worship services I attended contained little or no healing touch, I began asking why. I heard the following answers from both ministers and church members:

It's superstitious.
What if it doesn't work?
God meant for only Jesus to heal.
People should go to doctors, not church, for healing.

These answers reveal a lack of effective vocabulary for discussing healing ministry. They also reveal a more serious problem: an uneasiness with the whole notion of healing ministry. This dis-ease stems from the mind/body split discussed in chapter 2. We are not immune from its effects even in worship. It is as if we must leave our bodies outside. We design worship that requires a minimum of physical involvement. Except for ordination of church leaders and clergy, we never expect to receive laying on of hands to support us through life's trials.

However, if we stop for a moment to think about what Christian means, we will discover that we cannot let go of healing touch without denying who we are. The word Christ comes from the Greek *chriein,* "to anoint." The act of anointing (chrismation) with oil (chrism) served two main purposes in biblical times. It was used to consecrate kings, priests, prophets, or temple objects (Ex. 28:41; 29:7,21; 30:22–33) and to aid in caring for the sick and wounded (Isa. 1:6; Luke 10:35), and, after death, the body (Mark 16:1). Technically, laying on of hands was used to convey power and authority to those who would mediate the Spirit and shalom to the people of God (Num.

27:18, 23; Acts 6:6; 8:17). However, laying on of hands was also used along with rituals of anointing (Ex. 29:15, 19) and in ministry to the sick (Mark 5:23).[1]

These consecration rituals and healing practices gave Jesus a reference point for understanding his mission in terms of "the anointed," or the Christ (Luke 4:18). The New Testament does not record that Jesus claimed to be the Christ. Nonetheless, his disciples first took the name Christians in Antioch (Acts 11:26). Soon many more would bear the name Christian, not only from the trials they suffered in Christ's name (1 Peter 4:16) but also from the touch that welcomed them into the community of faith and identified them as "the anointed ones" (2 Cor. 1:21; 1 John 2:27).

In light of how the language of anointing has shaped our historical identity, we should not ignore the fact that since the Reformation we Protestants have taken a path that generally leaves these rituals behind. We no longer appreciate the medicinal and many other purposes for which oil was used so widely in ancient Mediterranean cultures. Indeed, since people seeking health today look to pharmacies, hospitals, or counseling centers, church historians William A. Clebsch and Charles R. Jaekle wonder "whether or how [healing touch in liturgy] is to be expressed at a time when its historical forms may well be beyond the possibility of resuscitation."[2]

We must remember that the Reformers who warned against using "accursed unction"[3] lived in a time when society was overgrown with the accouterments of religion. Today the reverse is true. Secular society depends on empirical evidence and avoids the symbols of the spiritual domain. This tendency demonstrates once again our splitness. At the same time it underscores the need for ritual symbols and signs that speak of wholeness. Today, writers of liturgical resources believe that "recovery of those signs from our broader Christian heritage that are rich in theological significance [such as laying on of hands and anointing] can mark the presence of God in our day and link us with the faith tradition of the centuries. Such worship will once again unite our bodies with our minds."[4]

How, then, is heart/hand coordination to be expressed in worship? What is our intention? How do we take into account the varied expectations of the gathered community? What guidelines are important to remember in a liturgical setting?

Intentions for Using Healing Touch in Liturgy

It is clear from the earliest liturgical records that arrangements were made to continue the healing ministry of Jesus in various forms of healing touch.[5] Members would carry home the oil blessed by the bishop as well as portions of the Lord's Supper. They would begin each day with the symbols of bread and wine and use oil for anointing the sick as needed.

To understand the intent behind this action, it is essential to remember that the blessing of the oil occurred immediately before the Lord's Supper as part of the offering and thus after the rituals of baptism. In the sacrament of baptism the worshipers would have witnessed the use of oil for exorcisms and anointings, water for cleansing, and laying on of hands for confirmation. Since the blessing of oil for healing touch comes out of this liturgical backdrop, it is the sacrament of baptism that we must examine for the meaning and intention of healing touch.

Baptism was the primary drama that shaped the early church's main Easter event (see chapter 2). Out of this ritual unfolded three main themes: (1) repentance and purification symbolized by exorcism with oil and washing with water, (2) laying on of hands and anointing with oil to confirm the presence of the Holy Spirit and empower the believer to be a faithful Christian, and (3) partaking of the Lord's Supper to celebrate full membership in the body of Christ. Thus the intent of clergy using touch in these services was to turn the catechumenates away from darkness and wash them clean of impurities, to mark them in close identity with Christ and apply the power of the Holy Spirit, and to feed them as a nourishing welcome into membership and ministry of the community of faith.[6] Liturgical scholars refer to the overall form of early Christian worship as an initiation shaped by the threefold action of baptism, confirmation, and communion.[7]

Unfortunately, the history of Christian liturgy is all too often the story of how the original integrity of worship became fragmented. Baptism was minimized, along with its rich tactile symbolism and its connection with confirmation and communion.

As early as the fifth century in the Western church, only bishops could officially administer the oil and laying on of hands associated with confirmation.[8] Consequently, this middle portion of the liturgy was reserved for occasions when the bishop could be present. Eventually, confirmation became a separate ritual in the Roman church, competing with baptism as a rite of passage into Christian community. Further fragmenting occurred when the Reformers, in their zeal for the basics, designed worship services in which the confirmation ritual with its gestures of touch was given little, if any, liturgical role. Baptism was left as a "sprinkling" or "naming" ceremony.

Only in recent decades has the liturgical movement sought to recover the integrity of Christian worship flowing from the waters of baptism as the pivotal initiating and consecrating action of the church. Modern liturgical scholars conclude that, whether infants, children, or adults are being baptized, the intent is a total consecration of the person to the mysteries of Christ's life, death, and resurrection, to the Spirit, and to the church's life and ministry. So central and formative is this act that all others parts of worship, including the Lord's Supper, flow out of and relate to it. In *Worship in the Community of Faith,* Harold Daniels writes:

> Each time we confess our sins and accept cleansing of God's forgiveness, we renew the ethical change of which the cleansing waters of Baptism are a sign. Each time we affirm our faith in the words of the creed, we renew our commitment to the faith rooted in the triune God to whom we were joined in Baptism. Each time we come to the Lord's Table, we renew the covenant into which we were baptized.[9]

Given the archetypal position baptism occupies in worship, we can see how all forms of liturgical touch relate in some way to our baptismal consecration to Christ and Christian community.

The kiss of peace (1 Peter 5:14) originally came right before the offering of bread and wine and continues to be placed after baptism and before the Lord's Supper. It emphasizes the baptismal theme of examining one's life, making peace before bringing gifts to the altar (Matt. 5:23), and welcoming one another to the fellowship.

The practice of laying on of hands to ordain persons to positions of leadership is based squarely on the fact that church leaders are drawn from a body of believers who are already ordained as a "royal priesthood" (1 Peter 2:9) by virtue of their one baptism in Christ. "Every ministry of the church derives its meaning and validation from the sacrament of baptism. Baptism is the ordination of the Christian to the continuing ministry of Jesus Christ."[10] In Orthodox liturgies, those who are baptized receive all the signs associated with ordination—the laying on of hands, oil, tonsure, and a white robe.[11]

Gestures of healing touch, such as laying on of hands, anointing with oil, and signing of the cross, are meant to strengthen members of the body of Christ so they might "reclaim all that baptism promises both in life and death."[12] Pastoral care educator Elaine Ramshaw writes that "the echoes of baptism in touch or word or oil . . . provide a paschal framework for the experience of suffering and death."[13] This intention is precisely the reasoning behind the pastoral instruction we find in the early church. Caesarius of Arles (470–543) advised:

> As often as one is taken by sickness . . . let him get to church and receive the Body and Blood of Christ and be anointed by priests with blessed oil. Let them ask the priests and deacons to pray over them in Christ's Name, which will bring them both health of the body and the remission of sins. For the Lord has been pleased to promise this through His Apostle James.[14]

Caesarius's advice ensured that the gesture of healing touch was never intended as a magical cure separate from the meanings of Christian worship. Indeed, even at bedside, "healing anointing is," as pastoral counselor Dennis J. Hughes reminds us, "for restoring the health of the person *and* the community in order that both may serve God with full vigor."[15] In Hughes' summary of the intended meanings of healing touch in liturgy, notice the prevalence of baptismal themes:

> That we belong to the Anointed One and in the community of the anointed ones; that we have been claimed, marked, and set apart as God's own children; that our sins are forgivable and forgiven; that our pain and sickness matter to God and to God's people; that there is a healing balm for our woundedness and a caring community for our loneliness.[16]

Expectations Surrounding the Use of Healing Touch in Liturgy

Given the profound intentions of healing touch, we might wonder whether we should offer it at all. Who could possibly understand, much less live out, its holistic implications? For that matter, contemplating the awesome ramifications of the initial rite from which healing touch derives its meaning, we might exclaim as did the 184th (1972) General Assembly of the United Presbyterian Church, "How dare we *baptize* anyone?"[17]

The truth is that though the intent of baptism and healing touch is to unite (or reunite) one's total life to Christ and Christian community, the power of these rituals is neither magical nor does it lie in some perfect vow-keeping capacity within believers. At most throughout our lives, we are, as the *Westminster Larger Catechism* puts it, "improving our baptism."[18] Therefore, we might expect to benefit from healing touch in liturgy only as it complements our dependence on God's faithfulness to supply the grace we need in our lives.

The shape of the liturgy itself addresses this expectation. In essence, baptism and healing touch are originally linked with confirmation and the Lord's Supper. Baptism gives us birth into Christian community. Laying on of hands and anointing with oil confirms us in a healthy dependence on the Holy Spirit. The eucharist sustains us throughout the journey of faith, with all its pains and pleasures.

The model for this pattern is consistent in the synoptic Gospels. Jesus' baptism (Matt. 3:13–17; Mark 1:9–11; Luke 3:21–22) sets him apart for God's purposes. A wilderness period follows (Matt. 4:1–11; Mark 1:12–13; Luke 4:1–13), into which Jesus is led by the Spirit. There he confirms his allegiance to God's call over against tempting alternatives. Finally, he returns to inaugurate his ministry, announcing the kingdom of God (Matt. 4:17; Mark 1:14–15; Luke 4:14–15).[19]

Early Christian worship followed this pattern. The oil of exorcism and washing (or immersion) in water in the name of the triune God recalled John's baptism of repentance. In the next (middle) segment, the bishop laid on hands and anointed with oil to confirm one's allegiance to Christ's call and to strengthen one's commitment by the power of the Holy Spirit. Finally, by receiving communion one was continually nourished and prepared to go forth into the world in service to Christ. The first two segments were onetime "birthings" and "sealings." Communion, as well as healing touch, would be ongoing rituals reflecting God's never-ending provision of grace for the fulfilling of the vows and promises made in baptism and confirmation.

Implicit in baptism, then, is the expectation that we will continually need to rely on God's grace to form and re-form us into the kind of people we were baptized to become. In short, baptism expects our lives in Christ to be an ongoing healing (whole-making) process. Thus, the threefold pattern of the liturgy that unfolds from baptism bears the familiar marks of healing process (see chapter 3).

Historically, we have tended to use metaphors other than healing to guide our thinking about the way worship reflects the drama of God's mighty acts: deliverance, redemption, reconciliation, liberation. These metaphors emphasize the important historical and communal nature of God's action. But these metaphors also depend heavily on concepts derived from the sphere of law and social contract. As essential as these references are for articulating revealed truth, no metaphor gets as close to the bodily realities of incarnational truth as healing.

Notice the two crucial expectations that the metaphor of healing keeps before us as we seek to understand Christian worship. We expect that believers will inevitably face times of testing when their faith and sense of well-being (health and salvation) are threatened. We also expect the liturgy of Christian community to engage us in a wholemaking healing experience. To overlook these expectations in worship tends to widen the split between mind and body and subtly diminishes our appreciation of the other theological themes worship dramatizes. Nevertheless, healing will always remain basic if we intend for worship to remain Christian. Just as the sick and suffering met the outstretched hand of Jesus, so in his church do we expect to find a continuation of his mission through healing touch offered in his name. As pastoral theologian Adolf Knauber puts it, "the anointing of the sick is to be viewed as a quite 'normal' recurring . . . form of [liturgical] encounter with Christ." [20]

We easily fall short of both expectations we have just identified. How many congregations truly expect worship to be a healing experience that takes into account the intimate and inseparable connections between body, mind, and spirit? More likely than not, our wordiness in the pulpit and immobility in the pews separate chancel from nave as effectively as we split our minds from our bodies in many other ways. In effect, we build in the sanctuary a protective shield against those who feel that their only hope for healing is to be touched by Christ's hands through his servants.

By the same token, how many of us anticipate that God's Spirit will lead us into wilderness times? Without that expectation we have no felt need for a healing ministry. Thus we end up expecting worship to be like TV—leading us into hypnotic trances that distract us from painful issues in our lives. Healing touch would awaken us from such restricted states of consciousness. Maybe that is why we avoid it like the plague.

If we are honest about the struggles that faith in Christ brings into our lives, every one of us will have to confess sooner or later that the suffering—and sometimes even the joy—seems too heavy to bear. Indeed, all God's reality inside us and outside "groans," as Paul says. We are always in need of the "spatio-temporal embodiment" [21] of the divine hand upon us.

Expressing such a need in the gathered community of faith is not an outmoded feature of worship. Neither does it demonstrate a lack of faith. Rather, it is the essence of faith's expectation. Accepting healing touch in worship is the liturgical equivalent to the basic and ongoing decision made by members of twelve-step programs: to admit powerlessness in relation to whatever threatens to undo us. *It is a realistic and natural expectation for Christians that from time to time we will feel the need to receive healing touch.*

Providing healing touch in symbolic liturgical action does not mean the church controls the healing process or even understands it completely. Rather, through the patterns and meanings of worship we participate in God's action to mold and reshape us every step of the way. As Methodist minister James K. Wagner sums it up, "we want to cooperate with the love of God in the healing process." [22] *It is natural and realistic for Christians to expect their liturgy to contain historical symbols and gestures, such as healing touch, that facilitate healing process.*

If we take these expectations seriously, what healing can be said to occur? What do we accomplish in liturgies that model and facilitate healing process? Consider, for example, a member who contracts lung cancer from years of smoking. The cancer is diagnosed as a fast-growing type, and the man is given only a few months to live. The event radically disrupts his life. He feels guilty about leaving his family and very angry toward himself. Subconsciously, he alleviates his depression by turning his anger toward God. He accepts the reality of his cancer and its consequences. However, even with the best pastoral counseling he cannot shake his anger. He sees clearly how his anger stands between him and God. Intuitively, he requests help from his pastor in the form of prayers with laying on of hands. What can the man and the church expect from such a ministry?

It is reasonable to expect that healing touch would communicate God's forgiveness, especially in terms of acceptance of the man's anger. It would also dramatize Christ's presence with him even through death. Especially if healing touch is received along with communion, it would emphasize fellowship in the body of Christ—a reminder of the bonds of love from which nothing in all creation can separate us. We can expect that as a result of becoming open to these meanings the man will be less fearful of God, less anxious in his personal relationships, and more hopeful of the future according to the promises of God.

We might also note the real possibility that the man's recently expressed anxieties and fears (triggered by the onset of the disease) may in fact have been old, unresolved problems against which he protected himself with his addictive behavior in the first place. If so, we could expect that addressing these issues, even at so late a date, might facilitate a healing process at some core level in his psyche.

Should we expect or even hope for remission of the cancer through healing touch? After all, if Jesus rose from the dead, everything is possible. A Christocentric answer demands that we put all possibilities before God: "Father, if you are willing, remove this cup from me" (Luke 22:42). In the case of the man with cancer, we might interpret his anger as similar to the first part of Jesus' prayer in the garden of Gethsemane. If healing touch has helped the man see his anger as an acceptable part of his relationship with God, the man might find other creative uses for his anger. According to the work of Bernie Siegel with exceptional cancer patients, the feisty patient who does not suppress anger is more apt to have a life that is longer and of better quality with (sometimes through) this disease.[23] So it is not wrong to bring to God one's earnest petitions.

However, if Jesus is our example in this matter we can see

right away what our problem may be in expecting a miracle of physical cure. Unlike Jesus, we have a profound proclivity to expect a miracle through some particular means, such as a healer, touch, or visualization. Furthermore, loading all our hopes onto a miracle—especially for a physical cure—can easily blind us to other areas of our lives in which God is bringing about healing during the most severe crisis. We tend to expect only the physical cure and forget the rest of Jesus' prayer: "Yet, not my will but yours be done."

If hope for remission of cancer becomes the doctor's, family's, or patient's focal point, healing ministry for this man may miss the other factors we have mentioned that are just as important, if not more so, than the disease and even his death. In addition, such a restricted focus would exclude problems arising in others—the man's family and the larger family of his church—who also figure in the crisis of faith at this time.

Addressing this whole constellation of concerns are the various symbols of Christian liturgy, especially forms of healing touch. For example, the laying on of hands and the signing of the cross on the forehead reconfirm the sense of God's acceptance and blessing, the Spirit's presence, and oneness with Christ in his life, death, and resurrection. These meanings will always speak to the whole man as well as his church. Maintaining this holistic perspective is what distinguishes healing ministry from faith cures or faith healing. Nowhere in the New Testament does it say the church is responsible for curing its members. However, it does ask us to pray for and with one another and to offer healing touch to those in life situations that threaten their sense of belonging to the body of Christ.[24]

The Iona Community in Scotland continually clarifies the expectations of worshipers by a statement included in their bulletins on Service of Prayer for Healing. It is worth quoting at length as a fitting summary to our discussion of expectation surrounding the use of healing touch in liturgy:

The New Testament tells us clearly not only to pray for the sick, but to lay our hands on them as we pray, and Jesus himself did

this many times. We know that in our daily lives, it is often touch
. . . that lets us know that we are loved. Touch, often more than
words, is a way of giving physical expression to our prayers and
concerns for each other. Those coming forward for prayer
for healing may not be ill physically—our past experience of
hurt, our tangled emotions, and our inability to forgive and to
receive forgiveness all make us less than whole and in need of
healing. . . .

Through the love and care of us all, God can act . . . healing
and restoring. We trust God to answer our prayers for healing,
but we do not know how or when our prayers will be answered.
We simply trust God to act in love for us, out of a deeper knowledge of our needs than we ourselves have. . . .

In this ministry of healing, we are in no sense rejecting the
work of medicine, which is also the gift of God. Prayer is not an
alternative, but a complement to other forms of healing, and a
recognition that healing comes in many ways, and is finally concerned with wholeness and not simply cure.[25]

Guidelines for Using Healing Touch in Liturgical Settings

Primed with intentions and expectations that are biblically
based and pastorally sound, we will find it much easier to arrange for healing touch to be a regular, visible part of worship.
The following five guidelines are helpful in reclaiming healing
touch in liturgical settings.

First, *healing touch is an integral part of healing ministry.* It
is therefore neither an occasional or seasonal emphasis nor a
strategy toward other goals the church may support. It is not a
commodity to be marketed to a public for which the church
does not intend to provide ongoing pastoral care. The occasion
for healing touch arises out of members' needs for restoration
of their faith and relationships in faith community. As these occasions inevitably arise, healing touch needs to be a regular part
of liturgy that reflects the church's obedience to Christ's healing ministry.

Second, *healing touch is not the exclusive right (or rite) of clergy, church officials, or even those who have a "gift of heal-ing"; rather, it is an expression of healing ministry that belongs to the whole church.* Since ordained or elected leaders repre-sent the whole church, it is natural to designate healing touch as one of their official liturgical and pastoral responsibilities. Clearly this is the model in James 5:14–16. But nowhere in the New Testament do we read that healing touch is inherent in leadership positions, nor do we find prohibitions against its use by members other than church leaders. Restricting this function to bishops was, as we have seen, the historical step that led eventually to its disappearance.

It is time we made room in liturgy not only for those who feel called to the ministry of word and sacrament, music, art, and movement but also for those who would provide touch as an expression of healing ministry. The early church blessed and provided oil for its members to use in rituals of healing as needed. The Iona Community in its healing service invites to the Lord's Table anyone who wants to provide laying on of hands as well as those who want to receive it. I visited one church that has a weekly Wednesday evening communion with laying on of hands for healing. After the service, members gather in the fellowship hall for dessert and intercessory prayer for those about whom they have abiding cares and concerns. Another church commissions for a "healing team" members who, after completing a training course, assist the clergy with prayer and laying on of hands in services of healing.[26] Since we do not control the Spirit's gifts, we need to be creative when they appear. It is entirely appropriate for any church member—especially in churches where no healing touch is offered—to feel the need for this gesture and to request the church to exam-ine its forms of healing ministry with an eye to reclaiming the church's forgotten language of healing touch.

Third, *reclaiming healing touch requires an honest review of how the church presently conducts its liturgy.* As healing touch gathers its meanings from the context of baptism–confirmation–communion, congregations who want to reclaim this gesture would do well to look at how they presently conduct worship. I suspect most liturgical practices and settings rarely encourage participants to make meaningful connection between these three basic components. As a result we become less familiar with initiational, transformational, and healing processes. Separation of confirmation from baptism and communion causes confusion. The baptistry's near invisibility and its scarcity of water reduce the value of its symbolism. It is debatable whether the clergy's and officers' parade of the elements to the pews tends more to display their leadership positions than to unite everyone in a communal action. In the Lord's Supper the sedentary posture of worshipers reduces a sense of participation in any kind of process, much less a healing one. This mode literally rules out the kind of healing touch historically associated with communal interaction around the Lord's Table.[27] The infrequency of the sacraments tends to make them seem strange and unfamiliar to the congregation. An honest review of worship often reveals the startling fact that there is little if any space or time for healing touch.

Fourth, *reshaping liturgy to include healing touch requires joint participation of those responsible for worship, pastoral care, and education.* Taking healing touch seriously teaches us once again about the inseparability of worship, pastoral care, and education. If healing touch is to be a genuine expression of compassion and not merely a trendy liturgical fixture, it will require thorough research and a continual monitoring of the way the church integrates its ritual and pastoral care. (See Bibliography and Resources for a list of resources that address historical and pastoral issues of healing touch in liturgical settings.)

Fifth, *healing touch in liturgy may be the only way some persons in difficult life situations may "hear" the gospel in worship.* I have often witnessed the power of healing touch in a variety of medical facilities. Patients have told me many stories of times when their doctor or nurse "just sat and held my hand and listened."

What has come as a surprise, however, is that now I am working outside settings of hospital chaplaincy I continue to hear these stories. Frequently, upon finding out that I do massage, someone will reach into his or her past and tell me about the time a parent or nurse "rubbed my back" and how much that meant. Somewhere in our psyche we have a special place reserved for these touch memories. Often they are landmarks that identify significant moments in our healing journeys.

I believe, also, that people take note when this special place is empty. One Sunday at worship a woman stood up during the moment for sharing and said, "Today marks the anniversary of my husband's death. I'm feeling a little shaky. If you have a touch or some hugs I could sure use them." After the service she received many warm embraces. It said a great deal about the church that she felt free to express this need. However, it might have said even more about the church and its message had the woman been able simply to come forward during the service to receive the comfort of Christ through the outstretched hands of his servants. How many others had similar needs but did not have the strength to express them? A healing touch may be the only means of grace for more people than we realize. Reminding us of our baptism in Christ, touch reconnects us to the solid Rock of our faith when other sources of strength are lost.

Speaking of touch rituals as "echoes of baptism," pastoral educator Elaine Ramshaw insightfully concludes that "though this is neither cure nor answer (the resurrection does not erase the cross), it is at least a connection with the life of God hidden in our wounded lives."[28] Thus for people who are sometimes overwhelmed by their empty spaces or who believe they are beyond reach, healing touch announces Emmanuel, "God with us." Providing this good news is the joy of healing touch.

Epilogue

Recently I visited Thailand to study Thai traditional massage. This discipline has been handed down through many generations by Buddhist monks. I wanted to find out what it was like to live in a culture in which an intentional form of healing touch was directly connected to and supported by the official clergy. The lesson I learned came not at the Wat Po Temple, where I received massage training, but a few blocks away in the National Museum at Bangkok. There I stood, a Christian in a Buddhist country listening to a Jewish guide talk about a Hindu sculpture.

She told us that, according to a legend from India, the quality of life at one time dramatically declined. Finally, the conditions for life on earth became so deplorable that Shiva, god of destruction, decided to burn it all up. So with the heat of his third eye he did so. Vishnu, god of preservation, heard about this after the destruction had occurred. All he could do was bring rain to put out the fire. Then, in total darkness, he lay down to figure out what to do. But he fell asleep.

The sculpture we observed in the museum depicts the sleeping Vishnu stretched out on the back of an aquatic beast, part crocodile and part lion. He is attended by two celestial helpers who massage his legs. From Vishnu's navel a stem grows upward and opens into a lotus blossom in the form of the head of Brahma, the creator god. The guide said, "It is not within Vishnu's power to make things new. Only by his connection with the Creator can he dream the new world."

A tourist asked, "Why are the celestial helpers massaging his legs?"

The guide answered, "Well, it's going to take Vishnu a long time to dream a new world. He'll need lots of healing energy."

It was then I saw more deeply into the wisdom of simple healing touch. We live in a time in which things truly have grown worse and worse. To reconcile minds with bodies, rich nations with poor ones, and humanity with its earth home is going to take a lot of energy. We may be tempted like one of Jesus' disciples to do too much and come to a dramatic rescue with the swords at our command (Luke 22:49–51). Or we may react as did Vishnu or Jesus' disciples and just fall asleep, overwhelmed at the magnitude of the task before us.

One hopes we will be more like the helpers at Vishnu's legs or like Jesus washing the disciples' feet. By laying on hands we do not will*fully* inflate our grandiosity, nor do we will-*less*ly freeze in the face of evil. Rather, we will*ing*ly provide the compassion and energy it takes to live toward visions of shalom only the Creator can give.

Reflection Sheets

Reflection Sheet No. 1: Healing Process

Instructions: Underline the words or phrases that best describe your life experience now. Afterward, discuss your self-description with a friend or counselor.

Faith.

Experiences strong feelings of anger, grief, guilt, and shame. Struggles with fear, depression, doubt, denial. Cries out with deep questions about the existence or presence of God, justice, fairness. Asks for help. Alternates between holding on and letting go of relationships, vocational identities, physical and mental faculties, self-images, God images. Alternates between receiving comfort, forgiveness, and help from family, friends, faith community, and even strangers and "going it alone." Confronts mortality. Lives day by day. Feels rejected, lonely, trapped, stuck, hopeless, worthless.

Hope.

Begins more realistic expression of deep feelings. Decreases alternation between holding on and letting go—for example, lets go of some resentments. Discovers new energies, capacities, insights. More willing to assess strengths and weaknesses accurately. Trusts emerging inner confidence and self-esteem. Experiments with trial-and-error methods. Develops a sense of humor. Makes new friends and support groups. Increases interest in communicating, sharing, playing, and being part of community. Pays closer attention to body, dreams, inner life, immediate surroundings, daily details. May even find life "richer." Apt to have mood swings, celebrating the highs of "progress" and bemoaning the lows of "reality." Exercises both patience and extreme impatience. May have surprising nightmares, setbacks, sudden fears such as suicidal thoughts. However, is open usually to be supported amid fears. Makes tentative plans. Expresses gratitude for any sense of movement through trials. Feels more thankful to God.

Love.

Transforms previous pains into compassion for others, especially for those in similar circumstances. Takes renewed interest in making commitments. Experiences a growing sense of purpose and meaning. Accepts mortality. Builds expectations out of learnings gained from trials. Often feels grateful even for the suffering endured. ("I wouldn't want to go through that again, but I wouldn't take the world for it either.") Finds creative ways to enhance personal and spiritual growth, to serve in the community, to clarify or change vocational goals. Able to forgive self, others, even God (in terms of old understandings of God). Embraces life's mysteries, paradoxes, pains, injustices. Relishes life's pleasure, goodness, beauty. Makes realistic assessment of weaknesses, limits, strengths, gifts. Lives out of expanding sense of community and relatedness (shalom). Sees God's hand guiding life, even using pain for good. Feels less judgmental, more accepting of others.

Reflection Sheet No. 2: Touch in a Pastoral Care Event

Instructions: When you have experienced a moment of pastoral care in which you sensed that touch played a significant role, use the questions below to help you reflect on that event (as soon afterward as possible).

OVERVIEW
Describe briefly the pastoral event.

INTENTION

Describe the intuitions, feelings, and motives out of which your touch emerged.

How did you feel as you entered into this encounter? Were you immediately aware of any intuitions? Were you aware of centering yourself? If so, how did you do this? Did touch help or hinder your sense of presence? What were your motives for touching? Did your motives or style of touching change as the episode progressed?

EXPECTATIONS

Describe the receiver's situation.

What was the receiver's problem or concern? What phase of healing process was evident? How did the receiver's situation affect the type of touch you used?

Describe how touch became part of the pastoral episode.

How did you hear the invitation to touch—verbal or nonverbal request, situational necessity, intuition, other? If you used your intuition, did you feel it was appropriate to check it out verbally with the receiver?

Describe the effects of your touch.

What did your touch communicate to the receiver? To you? To others? What indications were there that your message through touch was accurately received? What other effects did your touch have? Were they consistent with your pastoral objectives? What surprises occurred?

SETTING

Describe the setting of this episode.

How did the setting support or hinder the use of touch? What ritual aspects were part of touch—prayer, communion, other? Did you make any referral to professional touch therapies? If so, explain. What ongoing issues emerged out of this for you—control, boundaries, roles, resistances, other?

Examples of Ministries with Bodywork Therapy

Eleanor McKenzie DelBene, R.M.T., Ph.D., D.Min., P.O. Box 4, Trussville, AL 35173-0004. Phone: 205-655-7667.

Eleanor directs a retreat program called the Hermitage. Half of the directees are clergy, and half are helping professionals. Of these, 40 percent are recovering from sexual abuse and another 40 percent from alcohol-related problems. She offers a minimum of three two-hour sessions. Each session combines spiritual direction and bodywork. The first hour deals with issues that come from the directee's prayer life, dreams, or journal, portions of which might have been sent to her in advance. In the second hour the directee receives a massage. Afterward, Eleanor guides the directee in reflection on issues, images, and memories arising from the bodywork. Eleanor is a registered massage therapist and has a Doctor of Ministry in spiritual direction. With a Ph.D. in nutrition, her counseling is a holistic form of spiritual direction that she calls pneumasoma. She is a member of several professional organizations and has published articles about her work in journals on spiritual life.

Bradley James Enerson, D.Min., Trinity Lutheran Church, 346 West Pine Street, Lake Mills, WI 53551. Phone: 414-648-2717.

A Lutheran (ELCA) pastor, Bradley wrote his Doctor of Ministry thesis on "Massage as a Tool of Ministry within the Context of the Church" for Luther Northwestern Theological Seminary, St. Paul, Minnesota, 1990. The thesis reports the ongoing project Bradley directs at Trinity Church to train church members and others in the community to provide massage as a ministry to residents of the church's retirement center. In addition to basic massage skills, the training course includes "body theology" dealing with issues of shame, stress, sexuality, and spirituality. Bradley leads workshops for clergy and others on the use of massage in relation to the elderly, the dying, and those with AIDS. He has taken minicourses on massage at the University of Madison and provides about two massages a week in homes for persons with AIDS referred by the Madison AIDS Support Network. All who receive massage from Bradley or those he trains sign consent forms.

Richard Froehlig, M.Div., 3509 Dana Drive, Burnsville, MN 55337. Phone: 612-894-4582.

Richard is a Lutheran pastor (ELCA) who calls his work Healing Journeys Ministry. He directs this ministry full-time using space at Calvary Lutheran Church (Golden Valley, Minnesota), Easter Lutheran Church (Eagen, Minnesota), and his home. Richard offers leadership for individuals and groups in spiritual direction, having participated in a two-year program offered by Shalem Institute for Spiritual Direction in Washington, D.C. He also leads introductory seminars and weekend workshops for friends and family members on healing and wholeness through massage, acupressure, and centering prayer. Richard is a graduate of the Professional Massage School, St. Paul, Minnesota. He also coordinates Clergy Supporting Clergy, a volunteer support group of recovering clergy. Richard may give an introductory bodywork session to a counselee in spiritual direction; however, if the individual wants an ongoing program of bodywork therapy, Richard refers the person to another bodyworker. For persons in twelve-step programs Richard offers a free massage to those celebrating the Fifth Step as an "embodiment of absolution."

Dallas Landrum, M.Div., 10307 Crimson Tree Court, Columbia, MD 21044. Phone: 301-982-1519.

Dallas is a Presbyterian minister, former missionary to Iran, and now Interim Pastor at Lakeland Presbyterian Church, Columbia, Maryland. An accomplished carpenter, his interest in healing ministry has led him to use his hands in a variety of forms of bodywork—massage, craniosacral therapy, zero balancing, and Chinese foot massage, which he learned in Taiwan. As a bodyworker at St. Luke's Health Center in Baltimore in the mid 1980s, Dallas provided massage for abused women referred by physicians. Now, in private practice in Washington, D.C., and at his home in Columbia, half of Dallas's clients are survivors of sexual abuse. None of his parishioners are his clients. Generally, he thinks it best to keep bodywork and parish work separate functions. A "second parish" has emerged composed of his clients. As a result of his being a minister, his clients often become interested in talking about spiritual matters.

Brenda Lege, O. Carm., M.A., B.S.N., 4617 Carondelet Street, New Orleans, LA 70115. Phone: 504-895-1913.

A holistic health educator, Brenda directs the Center of Holistic Living in new Orleans. There she provides individual and small-group therapy using movement reeducation, stress management, massage therapy, nutrition education, and spiritual counseling. A third of her work is in conjunction with the staff of Blessing Place, a residential facility for sabbatical and renewal programs for men and women religious. She offers a holistically oriented approach, including massage, which speeds up other work that retreatants use, such as psychotherapy. If in her screening process Brenda determines that a person's problems are particularly intense or complex, she will make appropriate referrals and not attempt to address issues beyond her expertise. Half of her work involves traveling to present lectures, retreats, and workshops on holistic health and spirituality. She received her bodywork training in California from the institute of Educational Therapy in Berkeley, the Institute of Movement Psychology in Oakland, and the International Professional School of Bodywork in San Diego.

John McMahon, F.S.C., M.A., 635 Ocean Road, Narragansett, RI 02882. Phone: 401-782-6314.

A member of the Christian Brothers Center in Narragansett, John has been for most of his life a religious educator, spiritual director, and holistic counselor. He has worked in retreat centers for religious men and women in mid-life and for both religious and lay people in sabbatical programs. He completed training in massage therapy at the New Mexico Academy of Massage and Advanced Healing Arts in Santa Fe. He provides massage therapy for retreatants and private clients at Our Lady of Peace Spiritual Life Center in Narragansett. Retreatants use his bodywork as an adjunct to programs in spiritual direction offered by other staff members at the center. Though he does not combine spiritual direction with massage, clients who receive his bodywork and know of his pastoral skills often open up on a spiritual level. John also sees people solely for spiritual direction in a setting separate from massage. John is a member of the New England Holistic Counselors Association.

Keith Raske, M.Div., 932 Robert Street, Kirkwood, MO 63122. Phone: 314-984-9161.

Keith is an Episcopal priest in charge of Trinity Episcopal Church in St. James, Missouri. He studied the martial art of aikido, which led him to greater body awareness and eventually into bodywork. Keith graduated from the Kaleidoscope School of Massage Therapy in St. Louis and now spends some of his time on the faculty at that school. Using space in his home, he offers a private practice of integrated bodywork. These are group and individual sessions and workshops called "Coming to Our Senses." They feature meditative movement and hands-on therapy such as massage to develop body awareness. Most participants are either in a twelve-step group or in some other program of recovery from abuse. It is his policy not to do hands-on bodywork with members of his parish. "We're only as good as our boundaries," he says. Keith also works as a behavioral therapist at St. Anthony's Medical Center in St. Louis.

Susan Rikert, 112 San Pablo Avenue, San Francisco, CA 94127. Phone: 415-731-6576.

A member of the Friends Center of the San Francisco (Quaker) Meeting, Susan served four years as lay chaplain at

San Francisco General Hospital for indigents, refugees, and those with AIDS. There she provided seated on-site massage for her chaplaincy colleagues and trained them to do this for hospital staff. Also, she used therapeutic touch for infants in the neonatal intensive care unit under supervision of the head nurse. Now Susan goes into other hospitals, who pay her to give on-site massage to administrators, doctors, and nurses. She and her husband, Tom, formed Access Exchange International to build relationships between helping professionals in San Francisco and Moscow. She teaches on-site massage in Moscow to health care professionals and psychologists to build community and decrease stress. She developed Women in Transition, a program in which she listens for thirty to forty-five minutes to a woman talk about her divorce or impending death and then gives the woman a one-hour massage. Susan provides massage to participants at various retreat centers. She also leads retreats in California that include massage, free-form movement, music, and meditation at Mercy Center in Burlingame and the Quaker Retreat Center in Ben Lomond.

Dana Whitfield, 3914 Park Crest Drive, N.E., Atlanta, GA 30319. Phone: 404-255-6841.

A former dental hygienist, Dana graduated from the Atlanta School of Massage. She is a member of the Lutheran Church of the Apostles in Atlanta. As part of its Social Ministries Committee, Dana organized a Helping Hands Clinic in which area massage therapists volunteer one day a month to give free massage at the church for the elderly and the handicapped. In addition, she leads a chemical addiction support team providing drug and alcohol education for all ages. Dana offers "Christ-centered therapy" and coordinates monthly meetings of Christian massage therapists.

Notes

Introduction

1. The National Association of Bodyworkers in Religious Service (NABRS) was formed in 1990 for bodyworkers whose vocation includes some form of recognition by their faith communities. NABRS's purpose is to provide a nurturing network among its members and to assist the larger faith community in reclaiming healing ministry. For further information write Zach Thomas, 337 Tranquil Avenue, Charlotte, NC 28209.

2. John P. Dourley, *The Illness That We Are: A Jungian Critique of Christianity* (Toronto: Inner City Books, 1984).

3. Gai Eaton, "Perfecting the Mirror," *Parabola: The Body* 10, no. 3 (August 1985): 45.

4. Paul W. Pruyser, "The Master Hand: Psychological Notes on Pastoral Blessing," in *The New Shape of Pastoral Theology,* ed. William B. Oglesby, Jr. (Nashville and New York: Abingdon Press, 1969), 361.

5. Jürgen Moltmann, *God in Creation* (San Francisco: Harper & Row, 1985), 260.

Chapter 1. Called and Created to Touch

1. Walter H. Cuenin, "History of Anointing and Healing in the Church," in *Alternative Futures for Worship,* vol. 7, *Anointing of the Sick,* ed. Peter E. Fink, S.J. (Collegeville, Minn.: Liturgical Press, 1987), 65–81, quote from p. 72.

2. Charles W. Gusmer, *And You Visited Me: Sacramental Ministry to the Sick and the Dying* (New York: Pueblo Publishing Co., 1984), 21.

3. Morton T. Kelsey, *Healing and Christianity* (New York: Harper & Row, 1973), 165.

4. Ibid., 166, 167.

5. Mike Hamer and Nathaniel Mead, "Finding Heaven on Earth: Interview with Thomas Berry," *New Age Journal,* March/April 1990, 49–51, 135–40. Quote is on p. 136.

6. Quoted from René Descartes's *Discourse on Method* in a lecture, "Image of the Body in the Mind of the West," by Morris Berman, given at the Raphaelite Institute's Annual Retreat, June 8, 1990.

7. Renee Weber, "Philosophers on Touch," in *The Many Facets of Touch,* ed. Catherine Caldwell Brown (Skillman, N.J.: Johnson & Johnson Baby Products Co., 1984), 3–12.

8. For an extended discussion of the relevance of interpretive frameworks of the body for doing theology, see James B. Nelson, *Body Theology* (Louisville, Ky.: Westminster/John Knox Press, 1992), 41–54.

9. Kelsey, *Healing and Christianity,* 41.

10. For these references I am indebted to Kelsey, *Healing and Christianity,* 42–45.

11. Ibid., 50, 51.

12. Emma J. Edelstein and Ludwig Edelstein, *Asclepius: A Collection and Interpretation of the Testimonies* (Baltimore: Johns Hopkins University Press, 1945), 132–38.

13. Monica Sjoo and Barbara Mor, *The Great Cosmic Mother: Rediscovering the Religion of the Earth* (San Francisco: Harper & Row, 1987), 354.

14. Lester J. Kuyper, "Grace and Truth," *Interpretation: A Journal of Bible and Theology* 17, no. 1 (January 1964): 7.

15. Francis Brown et al., *A Hebrew and English Lexicon of the Old Testament* (Oxford: Clarendon Press, 1957), 373–74.

16. Kelsey, *Healing and Christianity,* 54.

17. Ibid., 79.

18. Ibid., 55–57. Kelsey uses the list compiled by Percy Dearmer, *Body and Soul* (London: Isaac Pitman & Sons, 1909).

19. Gusmer, *And You Visited Me,* 163.

20. Godfrey Diekman, "The Laying On of Hands in Healing," *Liturgy* 25 (1980): 7–10, 36–38. The author makes the following count regarding "touch"/"laying on of hands": Mark 12/6, Matthew 9/3, Luke 8/2. This reference is summarized by Gusmer, *And You Visited Me,* 163.

21. Gusmer, *And You Visited Me,* esp. chap. 1, "The Tradition of Anointing the Sick with Oil," 3–47.

22. Deane Juhan, *Job's Body: A Handbook for Bodywork* (Barrytown, N.Y.: Station Hill Press, 1987), 49, 50.

23. Quoted by Diane Ackerman, *A Natural History of the Senses* (New York: Random House, 1990), 73–74.

24. Juhan, *Job's Body,* 43–44.

25. Ibid., 45.

26. Ibid., 40.

27. Ibid., 13.

28. Sandra J. Weiss, "Parental Touch and the Child's Body Image," in *The Many Facets of Touch,* 130–38.

29. Juhan, *Job's Body,* 34.

30. See Kathryn Washington, "A Challenge to Somatics," *Creation Spirituality,* May-June 1991: 12–13.

31. Sharon McGeeney, "Touching Adult Children of Alcoholics," *Massage Therapy Journal,* Summer 1988, 30–33.

32. James B. Nelson, *The Intimate Connection: Male Sexuality, Masculine Spirituality* (Philadelphia: Westminster Press, 1988), 80.

33. Juhan, *Job's Body,* 18.

34. Ashley Montagu, *Touching: The Human Significance of the Skin* (New York: Harper & Row, 1978), 2.

35. Juhan, *Job's Body,* 29.

36. Ackerman, *A Natural History of the Senses,* 71, quoting Frederick Sachs, "The Intimate Sense of Touch," *The Sciences,* January-February 1988.

37. Martin L. Reite, M.D., "Touch, Attachment, and Health—Is There a Relationship?" in *The Many Facets of Touch,* 58–65. Also see M. Louise Bigger, Ph.D., "Maternal Aversion to Mother-Infant Contact," ibid., 66–70.

38. Montagu, *Touching,* 7–9.

39. Stanley E. Jones and A. Elaine Yarbrough, "A Naturalistic Study of the Meanings of Touch," *Communications Monographs* 52 (March 1985): 20, 51.

40. Ibid., 51.

41. Ibid., 51–52.

42. Janet F. Quinn, "Therapeutic Touch as Energy Exchange: Testing the Theory," *Advances in Nursing Sciences,* January 1984, 42–49.

43. Sara Beth Bowman, "The Effects of Empathic Touch and Expectations on Mood Change during Therapeutic Massage Treatment," unpublished doctoral dissertation, California School of Professional Psychology, Los Angeles, 1989, 195.

44. Nancy M. Henley, *Body Politics: Power, Sex, and Nonverbal*

Communication (Englewood Cliffs, N.J.: Prentice-Hall, 1977). See chap. 7, "Tactual Politics: Touch," 94–123.

45. M. Louise Bigger, "Maternal Aversion to Mother-Infant Contact," 68.

46. Juhan, *Job's Body,* 54.

Chapter 2. The Role of Touch in the Mind/Body Split

1. Andrew Kimbrell, "Body Wars: Can the Human Body Survive the Age of Technology?" *Utne Reader,* May-June 1992, 52, 53.

2. Morris Berman, *Coming to Our Senses: Body and Spirit in the Hidden History of the West* (New York: Simon & Schuster, 1989), 36.

3. Jules Older, *Touching is Healing* (New York: Stein & Day, 1982), 43–68.

4. Morton Kelsey, *Healing and Christianity* (New York: Harper & Row, 1973), 178–83.

5. Charles W. Gusmer, *And You Visited Me: Sacramental Ministry to the Sick and the Dying* (New York: Pueblo Publishing Co., 1984), 12.

6. Peter Brown, *The Body and Society: Men, Women, and Sexual Renunciation in Early Christianity* (New York: Columbia University Press, 1988), 441.

7. James C. McGilvray, *The Quest for Health and Wholeness* (Tübingen: German Institute for Medical Missions, 1981), 2–4. See also Darrel W. Amundsen and Gary B. Ferngren, "The Early Christian Tradition," in *Caring and Curing: Health and Medicine in the Western Religious Traditions,* ed. Ronald L. Numbers and Darrel W. Amundsen (New York: Macmillan Publishing Co., 1986), 47–52.

8. Brown, *Body and Society,* 441.

9. *The Apostolic Tradition of Hippolytus* (c.217) listed several vocations that had to be rejected in order to join the church, among which were charioteers, gladiators, soldiers, and military commanders. Ray C. Petry, ed., *A History of Christianity* (Englewood Cliffs, N.J.: Prentice-Hall, 1962), 30.

10. Margaret R. Miles, *Carnal Knowing: Female Nakedness and Religious Meaning in the Christian West* (Boston: Beacon Press, 1989), 44–45. Miles's chapter "Christian Baptism in the Fourth Century: The Conversion of the Body" (24–52) was the major source for my description of early Christian baptism. Another valuable resource is Marion J. Hatchett, *Commentary on the American Prayer Book* (New York: Seabury Press, 1980), 251–54.

11. Margaret R. Miles, *Fullness of Life: Historical Foundations for a New Asceticism* (Philadelphia: Westminster Press, 1981), 120.

12. Gusmer, *And You Visited Me,* 25.

13. Kelsey, *Healing and Christianity,* 203.

14. John Calvin, *Institutes of the Christian Religion,* ed. John T. McNeill (Philadelphia: Westminster Press, 1960), 4.19.18, 19; pp. 1, 467.

15. Richard Palmer, "The Church, Leprosy, and Plagues in Medieval and Early Modern Europe," in *The Church and Healing,* ed. W. J. Sheily (Oxford: Basil Blackwell, 1982), 82.

16. Darrel W. Amundsen and Gary B. Ferngren, "Medicine and Religion: Early Christianity through the Middle Ages," in *Health/Medicine and the Faith Traditions,* ed. Martin Marty and Kenneth L. Vaux (Philadelphia: Fortress Press, 1982), 128, 129.

17. Ibid., 118.

18. Marc Bloch, *The Royal Touch: Sacred Monarchy and Scrofula in England and France* (Montreal: McGill-Queen's University Press, 1973).

19. Kelsey, *Healing and Christianity,* 203.

20. Berman, *Coming to Our Senses,* 204. Italics his.

21. Fritjof Capra, *The Tao of Physics* (New York: Bantam Books, 1975), 45.

22. Berman, *Coming to Our Senses,* 238.

23. Ibid., 241.

24. Daniel J. Boorstin, *The Discoverers* (New York: Vintage Books, 1983), 674.

25. Older, *Touching is Healing,* 196.

26. Deldon Anne McNeely, Personal communication. See her book *Touching: Body Therapy and Depth Psychology* (Toronto: Inner City Books, 1987).

27. Jules Older, "Teaching Touch at Medical School," *Journal of the American Medical Association,* 252, no. 7 (August 17, 1984): 931–33.

28. In January 1989, I sent questionnaires to all clinical pastoral education centers and associated seminaries, 478 addresses, to determine the amount and kind of formal instruction on touch. A total of 157 completed questionnaires (30.4 percent) was returned. To check on the accuracy of these results, in January 1990, I sent 100 questionnaires to randomly selected centers and seminaries that had not responded to the first mailing. Of these, 41 completed questionnaires (41

percent) were returned. Approximately half reported that they offered instruction on touch. However, several qualified their answer by noting that they dealt with touch as it arose in the course of training. This method, of course, conforms to the pedagogical style of clinical pastoral education. Taking these factors into consideration, the survey revealed that the number of centers that *intentionally* dealt with touch was considerably less than half.

29. In examining all back issues of the *Journal of Pastoral Care* I found no article dealing with touch.

30. In *Services for Occasions of Pastoral Care,* Supplemental Liturgical Resource 6, prepared by the Ministry Unit on Theology and Worship, Presbyterian Church (U.S.A.) (Louisville, Ky.: Westminster/John Knox Press, 1990), I found no discussion of the subject of touch.

31. Quoted by Julie Dennison, "Not Less but a Different Kind of Touch," *Christian Century,* February 20, 1991, 200–203.

32. Bobette Perrone, Henrietta H. Stockel, and Victoria Krueger, *Medicine Women, Curanderos, and Woman Doctors* (Norman, Okla., and London: University of Oklahoma Press, 1989), 171. See also David F. Noble, *A World without Women: The Christian Clerical Culture of Western Science* (New York: Oxford University Press, 1992), 208–11.

33. Suzanne Gordon, *Prisoners of Men's Dreams: Striking Out for a New Feminist Future* (Boston: Little, Brown & Co., 1991). After thorough research on modern nursing in the United States, Gordon concludes that "many caregivers have come to feel that the greatest reward for their work—seeing the healing, empowering, life-enhancing benefits of human interaction—is now denied them," 147.

34. Older, *Touching is Healing,* 58.

35. Margaret R. Miles, *Practicing Christianity: Critical Perspectives for an Embodied Spirituality* (New York: Crossroad Publishing Co., 1989), 178.

36. Miles, *Carnal Knowing,* 51.

37. Margaret R. Miles, *Image as Insight: Visual Understanding in Western Christianity and Secular Culture* (Boston: Beacon Press, 1985), 64.

38. Miles, *Carnal Knowing,* 185.

39. Robert C. Fuller, *Alternative Medicine and American Religious Life* (New York: Oxford University Press, 1989). Fuller's explanation of the rise of Christian Science could apply to most if not all unorthodox movements: "Women suffered first and worst from the stresses of mod-

ern civilization and were thus predisposed to find something of existential relevance in [a] healing message," 79.

40. Ibid., 61.

41. Thomas E. Witherspoon, *Myrtle Fillmore: Mother of Unity* (Unity Village, Mo.: Unity Books, 1977).

42. Ann Braude, *Radical Spirits and Women's Rights in Nineteenth-Century America* (Boston: Beacon Press, 1989), 3.

43. Fuller, *Alternative Medicine,* 57.

44. Kelsey, *Healing and Christianity,* 237.

45. Berman, *Coming to Our Senses,* 108.

46. The American Massage Therapy Association (AMTA), organized in the late 1940s, had 1,500 members by the early 1980s. By 1992 it had grown to over 15,000 members. ("Annual Report, 1992," American Massage Therapy Association, 820 Davis, Suite 100, Evanston, IL 60201–4444.)

47. In the survey mentioned in note 28, over 75 percent of those who reported that they did *not* teach touch in any formal way said they thought they *should.*

48. Tim Weller, "Killings at 3 per hour, U.S. crime mushrooms," *Charlotte Observer,* March 13, 1991, 1.

49. The phrase is that of Ira Hutchison, professor of sociology at University of North Carolina—Charlotte, in an address to a workshop on "Family Violence," October 22, 1992, Charlotte, N.C.

50. Coleman McCarthy, "America's Routine Violence," *Charlotte Observer,* October 29, 1991, 9A.

51. Philip Greven, *Spare the Child: The Religious Roots of Punishment and the Psychological Impact of Physical Abuse* (New York: Alfred A. Knopf, 1991).

52. Ibid., 21.

53. Ibid., 14.

54. Ibid., 8.

55. The term is Alice Miller's. See her book *For Your Own Good: Hidden Cruelty in Child-Rearing and the Roots of Violence* (New York: Farrar, Straus & Giroux, 1983).

56. Pamela Cooper-White, "Soul Stealing: Power Relations in Pastoral Sexual Abuse," *Christian Century,* February 20, 1991, 196.

57. Karen Lebacqz and Ronald G. Barton, *Sex in the Parish* (Louisville, Ky.: Westminster/John Knox Press, 1991), 86.

58. Ibid., 80.

59. Peter Rutter, M.D., *Sex in the Forbidden Zone: When Men in*

Power—Therapists, Doctors, Clergy, Teachers, and Others—Betray Women's Trust (New York: Ballantine Books/Random House, 1989), 22.

60. Marie M. Fortune, "Betrayal of Pastoral Relationship: Sexual Contact by Pastors and Pastoral Counselors," in *Psychotherapists' Sexual Involvement with Clients: Intervention and Prevention,* ed. Gary Richard Schoener, et al. (Minneapolis: Walk-In Counseling Center, 1989), 82. See also Marie M. Fortune, *Is Nothing Sacred? When Sex Invades the Pastoral Relationship* (San Francisco: Harper & Row, 1989).

61. The research cited by Schoener, *Psychotherapists' Sexual Involvement,* p. 31, is S. H. Kardener, "Characteristics of 'Erotic' Practitioners," *American Journal of Psychiatry* 133 (1976): 1324–25,

62. Rutter, *Sex in the Forbidden Zone,* 223.

63. Dennison, "Not Less but a Different Kind of Touch," 200–203.

64. Cooper-White, "Soul Stealing," 196–97.

65. Ibid., 197.

66. Anne Wilson Schaef, *When Society Becomes an Addict* (San Francisco: Harper & Row, 1987), 50.

Chapter 3. The Language of Healing Touch

1. Walter Brueggemann, *Living toward a Vision: Biblical Reflections on Shalom* (Philadelphia: United Church Press, 1976), 182.

2. Gerald G. May, M.D., *Care of Mind/Care of Spirit: Psychiatric Dimensions of Spiritual Direction* (San Francisco: Harper & Row, 1982), 16.

3. Clyde W. Ford, *Where Healing Waters Meet: Touching Mind and Emotion through the Body* (Barrytown, N.Y.: Station Hill Press, 1989), 26.

4. Brueggemann, *Living toward a Vision,* 15.

5. For further discussion of these contemporaneous views of health see James N. Lapsley, *Salvation and Health: The Interlocking Processes of Life* (Philadelphia: Westminster Press, 1972), 59–67.

6. John A. Sanford, *Healing and Wholeness* (New York: Paulist Press, 1977), 15.

7. Greek philosophers listed faith, hope, and love (along with truth) as the basic elements of a genuine life; see Gerhard Kittel, ed. *Theological Dictionary of the New Testament* (Grand Rapids: Wm. B. Eerdmans Publishing Co., 1964), 2:520, 521. Paul used the framework of faith, hope, and love to outline the substance of Christian life (Rom.

5:1–5; 1 Corinthians 13) as did Augustine of Hippo: "Know thoroughly the proper objects of faith, hope, and love. For these must be the chief, nay, the exclusive objects of pursuit in religion." See Henry Paolucci, ed., *St. Augustine: The Enchiridion on Faith, Hope, and Love* (Chicago: Henry Regnery Co., 1961), 4.

8. "None of the stems [for 'faith'] is specifically religious in origin. In each the religious use seems to have secular roots." Gerhard Kittel, ed., *Theological Dictionary of the New Testament* (Grand Rapids: Wm. B. Eerdmans Publishing Co., 1986), 6:183.

9. Urban T. Holmes, *A History of Christian Spirituality: An Analytical Introduction* (New York: Seabury Press, 1981). The "three steps under different names go back to Origen, and before him to Philo, who probably got it from the Greeks" (p. 50).

10. Joseph Campbell, *Hero with a Thousand Faces* (Princeton, N.J.: Princeton University Press, 1949; 2d ed., 1968), 35.

11. Edward Edinger, *Ego and Archetype: Individuation and the Religious Function of the Psyche* (New York: Penguin Books, 1972), 183, 103.

12. Gerard Egan, *The Skilled Helper: A Model for Systematic Helping and Interpersonal Relating* (Monterey, Calif.: Brooks/Cole Publishing Co., 1975).

13. William Bridges, *Transitions: Making Sense of Life's Changes* (Reading, Mass.: Addison-Wesley Publishing Co., 1980); Arnold van Gennep, *Rites of Passage* (Chicago: University of Chicago Press, 1960). Also building on van Gennep's work is Victor Turner, *The Ritual Process: Structure and Anti-Structure* (Ithaca, N.Y.: Cornell University Press, 1969), and Robert L. Moore, "Ritual Process, Initiation, and Contemporary Religion," in *Jung's Challenge to Contemporary Religion,* ed. Murray Stein and Robert L. Moore (Wilmette, Ill.: Chiron Publications, 1987), 147–60.

14. James N. Lapsley, *Salvation and Health: The Interlocking Processes of Life* (Philadelphia: Westminster Press, 1972).

15. Pierre Wolff, *May I Hate God?* (New York: Paulist Press, 1966).

16. Gerald G. May, M.D., *Addiction and Grace* (San Francisco: Harper & Row, 1988), 57–63, 106.

17. Peter A. Campbell and Edwin M. McMahon, *Bio-Spirituality: Focusing as a Way to Grow* (Coulterville, Calif.: The Institute for Bio-Spiritual Research, 1990).

18. Kenneth L. Bakken and Kathleen H. Hofeller, *The Journey toward Wholeness: A Christ-Centered Approach to Health and Healing*

(New York: Crossroad Publishing Co., 1988); Bill J. Ratliff, *When You Are Facing Change* (Louisville, Ky.: Westminster/John Knox Press, 1989); John A. Sanford, *Healing and Wholeness* (New York: Paulist Press, 1977).

19. Zach Thomas, "Heart/Hand Coordination: Dynamics of Compassionate Touch," *Massage Therapy Journal,* Spring 1989, 20–23.

20. Anthony Stevens, M.D., *Archetypes: A Natural History of the Self* (New York: Quill Publishers, 1983), 5.

21. From a brief personal history submitted to the National Association of Bodyworkers in Religious Service in 1991. Used with permission.

22. From a brief personal history submitted to the National Association of Bodyworkers in Religious Service in 1991. Used with permission.

Chapter 4. The Intention of Touch in Pastoral Care

1. Karen Lebacqz and Ronald G. Barton, *Sex in the Parish* (Louisville, Ky.: Westminster/John Knox Press, 1991), 75–79.

2. Ibid., 158, 159.

3. Ibid., 236.

4. For this information I am indebted to Robert Johnson, Jungian analyst and author.

5. Jules Older, *Touching Is Healing* (New York: Stein & Day, 1982), 71.

6. Ibid., 71 (emphasis added).

7. Ibid., 200, 201.

8. Anne Stirling Hastings, *Reclaiming Healthy Sexual Energy* (Deerfield Beach, Fla.: Health Communications, 1991), 75.

9. David Calof's remarks were given in a workshop on "Working with Survivors of Abuse" presented in Charlotte, N.C., on March 7, 1992.

10. Deldon Anne McNeely, *Touching: Body Therapy and Depth Psychology* (Toronto: Inner City Books, 1987), 75.

11. Ibid., 97.

12. Robert L. Moore, "Archetypes of the Masculine Psyche," audiotapes of lecture, 1989.

13. Mirka Knaster, in a letter to the author, February 18, 1986.

14. Older, *Touching Is Healing,* 202.

15. David Eisenberg, M.D., *Encounters with Qi* (New York: W. W. Norton & Co., 1985).

16. See Elizabeth A. Rauscher, "Human Volitional Effects on a Model Bacterial System," *Subtle Energies* 1, no. 1 (1990): 21–41. For a discussion of the literature regarding research on laying on of hands, see Bernard R. Grad, "The Healer Phenomenon: What It Is and How It Might Be Studied," and Daniel J. Benor, M.D., "Psi Healing Research," in *Newsletter* (International Society for the Study of Subtle Energies and Energy Medicine) 2, no. 2 (Summer 1991).

17. Gerald G. May, M.D., *Addiction and Grace* (San Francisco: Harper & Row, 1988), 6.

Chapter 5. Expectations and Settings of Touch

1. See Deldon Anne McNeely's discussion of resistances in *Touching: Body Therapy and Depth Psychology* (Toronto: Inner City Books, 1987), 60–62.

2. Jules Older, *Touching Is Healing* (New York: Stein & Day, 1982), 241.

3. Joyce E. Pattison found in a comparison of two groups of counselors' clients that "clients who are touched engage in more self-exploration than clients who are not touched." "Effects of Touch on Self-Exploration and the Therapeutic Relationship," *Journal of Counseling and Clinical Psychology* 40, no. 2 (1973): 170–75; quote is on p. 171.

4. McNeely, *Touching,* 66.

5. For further information on "body-oriented" or "somatic" psychotherapy, contact the International Scientific Committee for Psychocorporal Therapy represented in the United States by Jack Painter, creator of Postural Integration and director of the International Center for Release and Integration in Mill Valley, California. For examples of ministry utilizing bodywork therapy, see Appendix B; see also Bibliography and Resources for information about professional associations and other resources.

6. Carl Dubitsky, O.B.T., L.M.T., "Three Paradigms, Five Approaches," *Massage Therapy Journal* 30, no. 3 (summer 1991): 21–23; co-authors: Patricia Benjamin, Raymond Castellino, Jeffrey Maitland, Steven Schenkman.

7. Ibid., 21.

8. Ibid.

9. Ibid.

10. Personal communication from psychosynthesis practitioners Jean Stewart, Charlotte, North Carolina, and Phyllis L. Clay, Stillpoint

Center for Spirituality, Independence, Missouri. See also Roberto Assagioli, *Psychosynthesis* (New York: Penguin Books, 1981), and John Weiser and Thomas Yoemans, *Psychosynthesis in the Helping Professions: Now and for the Future* (Toronto: Ontario Institute for Studies in Education, 1984).

11. Clyde Ford, *Where Healing Waters Meet: Touching Mind and Emotion through the Body* (Barrytown, N.Y.: Station Hill Press, 1989). See also by the same author *Compassionate Touch: The Role of Human Touch in Healing and Recovery* (New York: Simon and Schuster, 1993).

12. Malcolm Brown, *The Healing Touch: An Introduction to Organismic Psychotherapy* (Mendocino, Calif.: Life Rhythm, 1990), 218. See also Jack W. Painter, *Deep Bodywork and Personal Development: Harmonizing Our Bodies, Emotions, and Thoughts* (Mill Valley, Calif.: Bodymind Books, 1987).

13. Janet Travell, M.D., and David G. Simons, M.D., *Myofascial Pain and Dysfunction: The Trigger Point Manual* (Baltimore: Williams & Wilkins, 1983), xii.

14. Ibid.

15. These methods are commonly called "trigger point therapy" or "neuromuscular therapy." Many massage therapists learn these methods in certification programs such as those taught by Paul St. John, a student of Travell who founded and now directs the St. John Neuromuscular Pain Relief Institute in Largo, Florida.

16. Ida P. Rolf, *Rolfing: The Integration of Human Structures* (San Francisco: Harper & Row, 1977), 15.

17. Robert J. Timms and Patrick Connors, *Embodying Healing: Integrating Bodywork and Psychotherapy in Recovery from Childhood Sexual Abuse* (Orwell, Vt.: Safer Society Press, 1992).

Chapter 6. Healing Touch in Worship

1. Dennis J. Hughes, "Anointing and Prayers for Restoration of the Sick: Reclaiming a Biblical Mandate," *Reformed Liturgy and Music* 24, no. 3 (summer 1990): 136–39. Hughes discusses the difference between anointing in acts of consecration and anointing for purposes of healing. The latter serves to recall, not duplicate, the former.

2. William A. Clebsch and Charles R. Jaekle, *Pastoral Care in Historical Perspective* (Englewood Cliffs, N.J.: Prentice-Hall, 1964), 42.

3. John Calvin, *Institutes of the Christian Religion,* ed. John T. McNeill (Philadelphia: Westminster Press, 1960), 4.19.21; 1469.

4. Office of Worship for the Presbyterian Church (U.S.A.) and the Cumberland Presbyterian Church, *Holy Baptism and Services for the Renewal of Baptism,* Supplemental Liturgical Resource 2 (Philadelphia: Westminster Press, 1985), 60.

5. *The Apostolic Tradition,* from *Hippolytus: A Text for Students,* ed. Geoffrey J. Cuming (Nottingham: Grove Books, 1976), 11: "If anyone offers oil, [the bishop] shall render thanks in the same way as for the offering of bread and wine, not saying it word for word, but to similar effect, saying: O God, sanctifier of this oil, as you give health to those who are anointed and [*sic*] receive that with which you anointed kings, priests, and prophets, so may it give strength to all those who taste it, and health to all that are anointed with it."

6. Marion J. Hatchett, *Commentary on the American Prayer Book* (New York: Seabury Press, 1980), 252: "In this regard, the intention was similar to that in rituals of initiation in other communities."

7. Gerard Austin, *Anointing with the Spirit: The Rite of Confirmation: The Use of Oil and Chrism* (New York: Peublo Publishing Co., 1985); see chap. 6, esp. pp. 125–56.

8. R. R. Williams, "Laying on of Hands," in *A Theological Word Book of the Bible,* ed. Alan Richardson (New York: Macmillan Co., 1962), 127.

9. Harold M. Daniels, ed., *Worship in the Community of Faith* (Louisville, Ky.: Joint Office of Worship, 1982), 92.

10. Ministry Unit on Theology and Worship, *Services for Occasions of Pastoral Care,* Supplemental Liturgical Resource 6 (Louisville, Ky.: Westminster/John Knox Press, 1990), 14, 15.

11. J. G. Davies, ed., "Ordination," in *The Westminister Dictionary of Worship* (Philadelphia: Westminster Press, 1972), 287.

12. *Services for Occasions of Pastoral Care,* 37.

13. Elaine Ramshaw, *Ritual and Pastoral Care* (Philadelphia: Fortress Press, 1987), 65.

14. Cited by Charles W. Gusmer, *And You Visited Me: Sacramental Ministry to the Sick and the Dying* (New York: Pueblo Publishing Co., 1984), 16.

15. Hughes, "Anointing and Prayers," 138, emphasis added.

16. Ibid., 138.

17. Quoted by Harold M. Daniels, ed., *Worship in the Community of Faith,* 75, emphasis added.

18. "The Larger Catechism," *Our Confessional Heritage: Confessions of the Reformed Tradition with a Contemporary Declaration of*

Faith (Atlanta: Presbyterian Church in the U.S., 1978), Question 167, p. 134.

19. *Services for Occasions of Pastoral Care,* 15, 16. I am grateful to the authors of this book for drawing my attention to the relationship of the Gospel narratives to early Christian worship.

20. Adolf Knauber, *Pastoral Theology of the Anointing of the Sick: God's Healing,* trans. Matthew J. O'Connell (Collegeville, Minn.: Liturgical Press, 1975), 30A.

21. Ibid., 29A, quoting Karl Rahner, *The Church and the Sacraments,* trans. W. J. O'Hara (New York: Herder & Herder, 1963), 61, n.4.

22. James K. Wagner, *Blessed to Be a Blessing: How to Have an Intentional Healing Ministry in Your Church* (Nashville: Upper Room, 1980), 58.

23. Bernie Siegel, M.D., *Love, Medicine, and Miracales* (New York: Harper & Row, 1986).

24. Hughes, "Anointing and Prayers," 139. I am grateful to Hughes for this insight.

25. *The Iona Community Worship Book* (Glasgow: Wild Goose Publications, 1988), 35, 36.

26. Irene Perkins, "Building a Healing Team in the Local Church," *Weavings* 6, no. 4 (July-August 1991): 37–42.

27. For years Scottish Presbyterians were accustomed to receiving communion around "long tables" erected in the sanctuary. In the seventeenth century, the novel idea of carrying the elements to members in their seats was considered irreverent, a "mangling" of the sacraments and a practice at the fringes of Christianity. "The practice of abandoning the long tables and having the elements carried by the elders to the communicants in their pews seems to have been introduced in Scotland . . . in 1819." George B. Burnet, *The Holy Communion in the Reformed Church of Scotland, 1560–1960* (Edinburgh and London: Oliver & Boyd, 1960), 269.

28. Ramshaw, *Ritual and Pastoral Care,* 65.

Bibliography
and Resources

Historical and Theological Studies on Health and Medicine and Mind/Body Issues

Alster, Kristine Beyerman. *The Holistic Health Movement.* Tuscaloosa, Ala.: University of Alabama Press, 1989.

Berman, Morris. *Coming to Our Senses: Body and Spirit in the Hidden History of the West.* New York: Simon & Schuster, 1989.

Bloch, Marc. *The Royal Touch: Sacred Monarchy and Scrofula in England and France.* London: Routledge & Kegan Paul, 1973.

Brown, Peter. *The Body and Society: Men, Women, and Sexual Renunciation in Early Christianity.* New York: Columbia University Press, 1988.

Brueggemann, Walter. *Living toward a Vision: Biblical Reflections on Shalom.* Philadelphia: United Church Press, 1976.

Conger, John P. *Jung and Reich: The Body as Shadow.* Berkeley, Calif.: North Atlantic Books, 1988.

Dourley, John P. *The Illness That We Are: A Jungian Critique of Christianity.* Toronto: Inner City Books, 1984.

Fuller, Robert C. *Alternative Medicine and American Religious Life.* New York: Oxford University Press, 1989.

Kelsey, Morton T. *Healing and Christianity.* New York: Harper & Row, 1973.

McGilvray, James C. *The Quest for Health and Wholeness.* Tübingen: German Institute for Medical Missions, 1981.

Marty, Martin, and Kenneth L. Vaux, eds. *Health/Medicine and the Faith Traditions: An Inquiry into Religion and Medicine.* Philadelphia: Fortress Press, 1982.

Miles, Margaret R. *Augustine on the Body.* Missoula, Mont.: Scholars Press, 1979.

———. *Carnal Knowing: Female Nakedness and Religious Meaning in the Christian West.* Boston: Beacon Press, 1989.

———. *Fullness of Life: Historical Foundations for a New Asceticism.* Philadelphia: Westminster Press, 1981.

———. *Practicing Christianity: Critical Perspectives for an Embodied Spirituality.* New York: Crossroad Publishing Co., 1988.

Moltmann, Jürgen. *God in Creation: A New Theology of Creation and the Spirit of God.* San Francisco: Harper & Row, 1985.

Murphy, Michael. *The Future of the Body.* Los Angeles: Jeremy P. Tarcher, 1992.

Nelson, James B. *Body Theology.* Louisville, Ky.: Westminster/John Knox Press, 1992.

Noble, David F. *A World without Women: The Christian Clerical Culture of Western Science.* New York: Oxford University Press, 1992.

Numbers, Ronald L., and Darrel W. Amundsen, eds. *Caring and Curing: Health and Medicine in the Western Religious Traditions.* New York: Macmillan Publishing Co., 1986.

Perrone, Bobette, Henrietta H. Stockel, and Victoria Krueger. *Medicine Women, Curanderos, and Women Doctors.* Norman, Okla., and London: University of Oklahoma Press, 1989.

Ruether, Rosemary Radford. *Ecofeminism: Symbolic and Social Connections between the Oppression of Women and the Domination of Nature.* Loy H. Witherspoon Lectures in Religious Studies. University of North Carolina at Charlotte, 1991.

Sanford, John A. *Healing and Wholeness.* New York: Paulist Press, 1977.

Sheily, W. J., ed. *The Church and Healing.* Oxford: Basil Blackwell, 1982.

Sullivan, Lawrence E. *Healing and Restoring: Health and Medicine in the World's Religious Traditions.* New York: Macmillan Publishing Co., 1989.

Vaux, Kenneth L. *Health and Medicine in the Reformed Tradition: Promise, Providence, and Care.* New York: Crossroad Publishing Co., 1984.

Westberg, Granger E., ed. *Theological Roots of Wholistic Health Care.* Hinsdale, Ill.: Wholistic Health Centers, 1979.

Sociological, Psychological, and Clinical Studies of Touch

Blondis, Marion N., and Barbara E. Jackson. *Nonverbal Communication with Patients: Back to the Human Touch,* 2d ed. New York: John Wiley & Sons, 1982.

Brown, Catherine Caldwell, ed. *The Many Facets of Touch—The Foundations of Experience: Its Importance through Life, with Initial Emphasis for Infants and Young Children.* Skillman, N.J.: Johnson & Johnson Baby Products Co., 1984.

Greven, Philip. *Spare the Child: The Religious Roots of Punishment and the Psychological Impact of Physical Abuse.* New York: Alfred A. Knopf, 1991.

Gunzenhauser, Nina, ed. *Advances in Touch: New Implications in Human Development.* Skillman, N.J.: Johnson & Johnson Baby Products Co., 1990.

Henley, Nancy M. *Body Politics: Power, Sex, and Nonverbal Communication.* Engelwood Cliffs, N.J.: Prentice-Hall, 1977.

Juhan, Deane. *Job's Body: A Handbook for Bodywork.* Barrytown, N.Y.: Station Hill Press, 1987.

McGuire, Meredith B. *Ritual Healing in Suburban America.* New Brunswick, N.J., and London: Rutgers University Press, 1988.

McNeely, Deldon Anne. *Touching: Body Therapy and Depth Psychology.* Toronto: Inner City Books, 1987.

Miller, Alice. *For Your Own Good: Hidden Cruelty in Child-Rearing and the Roots of Violence.* New York: Farrar, Straus & Giroux, 1983.

Montagu, Ashley. *Touching: The Human Significance of the Skin.* New York: Harper & Row, 1978.

Older, Jules. *Touching Is Healing.* New York: Stein & Day, 1982.

Simon, Sidney. *Caring, Feeling, Touching.* Niles, Ill.: Argus Communications, 1976.

Yates, John. *A Physician's Guide to Therapeutic Massage: Its Physiological Effects and Their Application to Treatment.* Vancouver: Massage Therapists' Association of British Columbia, 1990.

Studies on Healing and Transformation Process

Bakken, Kenneth L., and Kathleen H. Hofeller. *The Journey toward Wholeness: A Christ-Centered Approach to Health and Healing.* New York: Crossroad Publishing Co., 1988.

Bridges, William. *Transitions: Making Sense of Life's Changes.* Reading, Mass.: Addison-Wesley Publishing Co., 1980.

Campbell, Joseph. *Hero with a Thousand Faces.* Princeton, N.J.: Princeton University Press, 1968.

Edinger, Edward. *Ego and Archetype: Individuation and the Religious Function of the Psyche.* New York: Penguin Books, 1972.

Egan, Gerard. *The Skilled Helper: A Model for Systematic Helping and Interpersonal Relating.* Monterery, Calif.: Brooks/Cole Publishing Co., 1975.

Fowler, James. *Faith Development and Pastoral Care.* Philadelphia: Fortress Press, 1987.

Fox, Matthew. *Original Blessing.* Santa Fe, N.M.: Bear & Co., 1983.

Gennep, Arnold von. *Rites of Passage.* Trans. Monika B. Vizedom and Gabrielle L. Caffee. Chicago: University of Chicago Press, 1960.

Holmes, Urban T. *A History of Christian Spirituality: An Analytical Introduction.* New York: Seabury Press, 1981.

Jung, Carl G. *The Collected Works of C. G. Jung,* vol. 12, *Psychology and Alchemy,* ed. W. McGuire. Princeton, N.J.: Princeton University Press, 1968, 227–41.

Kidd, Sue Monk. *When the Heart Waits.* San Francisco: HarperCollins, 1992.

Kreis, Bernadine, and Alice Pattie. *Up from Grief: Patterns of Recovery.* New York: Seabury Press, 1982.

Lapsley, James N. *Salvation and Health: The Interlocking Processes of Life.* Philadelphia: Westminster Press, 1972.

Lindemann, Erich. *Beyond Grief.* New York: Jason Aronson, 1979.

May, Gerald G. *Addiction and Grace.* San Francisco: Harper & Row, 1988.

Moore, Robert L. "Ritual Process, Initiation, and Contemporary Religion," in *Jung's Challenge to Contemporary Religion,* eds. Murray Stein and Robert L. Moore. Wilmette, Ill.: Chiron Publications, 1987, 147–60.

Nouwen, Henri J. M. *Reaching Out: The Three Movements of the Spiritual Life.* Garden City, N.Y.: Doubleday & Co., 1975.

Ratliff, J. Bill. *When You Are Facing Change.* Louisville, Ky.: Westminster/John Knox Press, 1989.

Turner, Victor. *The Ritual Process: Structure and Anti-Structure.* Ithaca, N.Y.: Cornell University Press, 1969.

Underhill, Evelyn. *Mysticism: A Study in the Nature and Development of Man's Spiritual Consciousness.* New York: E. P. Dutton, 1961, 167–75.

Wilbur, Ken. *The Atman Project: A Transpersonal View of Human Development.* Wheaton, Ill.: Theosophical Publishing House, 1980.

Resources on Bodywork Modalities and Organizations

Barstow, Cedar. *Tending Body and Spirit: Massage and Counseling with Elders.* Boulder, Colo.: Boulder School of Massage, 1985.

Brown, Malcolm. *The Healing Touch: An Introduction to Organismic Psychotherapy.* Mendocino, Calif.: LifeRhythm, 1990.

Drury, Nevill, ed. *The Bodywork Book.* San Leandro, Calif.: Prism Alpha, 1984.

Dychtwald, Ken. *Bodymind.* Los Angeles: Jeremy P. Tarcher, 1977.

Feldenkrais, Moshe. *Awareness through Movement.* New York: Harper & Row, 1972.

Ford, Clyde W. *Where Healing Waters Meet: Touching Mind and Emotion through the Body.* Barrytown, N.Y.: Station Hill Press, 1989.

———. *Compassionate Touch: The Role of Human Touch in Healing and Recovery.* New York: Simon & Schuster, 1993.

Jones, Frank Pierce. *Body Awareness in Action: A Study of the Alexander Technique.* New York: Schocken Books, 1979.

Kepner, James I. *Body Process: A Gestalt Approach to Working with the Body in Psychotherapy.* New York: Gardner Press, 1987.

Krieger, Dolores. *The Therapeutic Touch: How to Use Your Hands to Help or to Heal.* Englewood Cliffs, N.J.: Prentice-Hall, 1979.

Kurtz, Ron. *Body-Centered Psychotherapy: The Hakomi Method.* Mendocino, Calif.: LifeRhythm, 1990.

Licht, Sidney, M.D. *Massage, Manipulation, and Traction.* New Haven, Conn.: Elizabeth Licht, 1960.

Lowen, Alexander. *Bioenergetics.* New York: Penguin Books, 1975.

Marcus, Eric. *Gestalt Therapy and Beyond: An Integrated Mind-Body Approach.* Cupertino, Calif.: Meta Publications, 1979.

McNeely, Deldon Anne. "Body Therapy in Historical Perspective," in her *Touching: Body Therapy and Depth Psychology,* Toronto: Inner City Books, 1987, 21–58.

Older, Jules. "The Body Therapies," in his *Touching Is Healing.* New York: Stein & Day, 1982, 219–33.

Painter, Jack W. *Deep Bodywork and Personal Development: Harmonizing Our Bodies, Emotions, and Thoughts.* Mill Valley, Calif.: Bodymind Books, 1987.

Ray, Barbara. *The Reiki Factor: A Guide to Natural Healing, Helping, and Wholeness.* Smithtown, N.Y.: Exposition Press, 1983.

Rolf, Ida P. *Rolfing: The Integration of Human Structures.* San Francisco: Harper & Row, 1977.

Rosenberg, Jack L., Marjorie L. Rand, and Diane Asay, *Body, Self, and Soul.* Atlanta: Humanics, Ltd., 1989.

Smith, E.W.L. *The Body in Psychotherapy.* Jefferson, N.C.: McFarland & Co., 1985.

Smith, Fritz F. M.D. *Inner Bridges: A Guide to Energy Movement and Body Structure.* Atlanta: Humanics Ltd., 1986.

Timms, Robert, and Patrick Connors. *Embodying Healing: Integrating Bodywork and Psychotherapy in Recovery from Childhood Sexual Abuse.* Orwell, Vt.: Safer Society Press, 1992.

Travell, Janet G., M.D., and David G. Simons, M.D. *Myofascial Pain and Dysfunction: The Trigger Point Manual.* Baltimore: Williams & Wilkins, 1983.

Liturgical Resources

Austin, Gerard. *Anointing with the Spirit.* New York: Pueblo Publishing Co., 1985.

Daniels, Harold M., ed. *Worship in the Community of Faith.* Louisville, Ky.: Joint Office of Worship, 1982.

Davies, J. G., ed. *The New Westminster Dictionary of Liturgy and Worship.* Philadelphia: Westminster Press, 1986.

Fink, Peter E., ed. *Alternative Futures for Worship,* vol. 7: *Anointing the Sick.* Collegeville, Minn.: Liturgical Press, 1987.

Gusmer, Charles W. *And You Visited Me: Sacramental Ministry to the Sick and Dying.* New York: Pueblo Publishing Co., 1984.

Knauber, Adolf. *Pastoral Theology of the Anointing of the Sick,* trans. Matthew J. O'Connell. Collegeville, Minn.: Liturgical Press, 1975.

Ministry Unit on Theology and Worship. *Services for Occasions of Pastoral Care,* Supplemental Liturgical Resource 6. Louisville, Ky.: Westminster/John Knox Press, 1990.

Office of Worship for the Presbyterian Church (U.S.A.) and the Cumberland Presbyterian Church. *Holy Baptism and Services for the Renewal of Baptism,* Supplemental Liturgical Resource 2. Philadelphia: Westminster Press, 1985.

Ramshaw, Elaine. *Ritual and Pastoral Care.* Philadelphia: Fortress Press, 1987.

Wagner, James K. *Blessed to Be a Blessing: How to Have an Intentional Healing Ministry in Your Church.* Nashville, Tenn.: Upper Room, 1980.

Professional Associations

See Cherie Sohnen-Moe, *Business Mastery* (Tucson, Ariz.: Sohnen-Moe Associates, 1991), for a listing of nearly three hundred healing arts professional associations. For more detail about these and other groups, see the section "Health and Medical" in the *Encyclopedia of Associations.*

For a complete listing of massage and bodywork modalities, schools, organizations, periodicals, and supplies see Martin Ashley, *Massage: A Career at Your Fingertips* (Barrytown, N.Y.: Station Hill Press, 1992).

Information and Referral

For a description of bodywork modalities to help consumers make informed decisions about the type of bodywork most appropriate for their needs, see Mirka Knaster, *Discovering the Wisdom of the Body* (New York: Bantam Books, forthcoming).

For a listing of bodywork professionals in your area, call leaders of local bodywork associations. Headquarters for national associations of major methods mentioned in this book are:

American Massage Therapy Association, 820 Davis, Suite 100, Evanston, IL 60201-4444.
American Oriental Bodywork Therapy Association, 50 Maple Place, Manhasset, NY 11030.
American Polarity Therapy Association. P.O. Box 1517, Arlington, MA 02174.
Rolf Institute, P.O. Box 1868, Boulder, CO 80306.
Shiatsu Therapeutic Association of America, 602 Kailua Road, #205-B, Kailua, HI 96734.
Trager Institute, 10 Old Mill Street, Mill Valley, CA 94941.

Index